Praise for *The Spider's Strategy*

"Beyond the obvious, this is a great and pragmatic book, demonstrating the incredible power of Collaboration in action."

—*Jean-Francois Baril*
Senior Vice President, Nokia Corporation

"Though many have sought to unlock the secrets of creating learning organizations, few have succeeded. In *The Spider's Strategy*, Mukherjee provides the keys to the learning kingdom.... And he shows what it really takes to leverage the power of networks. It is that rare business book that deserves to be read from cover-to-cover."

—*Michael Watkins*, Author of *The First 90 Days: Critical Success Strategies for New Leaders at All Levels*

"Mukherjee beautifully weaves the ever-morphing web of technology, business, and organizational learning together and explains why both top executives and middle managers must care about their impact."

—*Sudipta Bhattacharya*
President, Invensys Wonderware

"About the time of the Nokia incident, the Toyota Group faced a similar situation in Japan and its actions were a good example of best practice—but in a setting of a local network, strong ties, and integral business architecture. I was not sure if a switch from a transactional mode to a knowledge sharing mode could happen in a global network with weaker ties and a modular business architecture. *The Spider's Strategy* convinced me that it is certainly possible—by building sense-and-respond capabilities, collaboration with network partners, organizational learning, and responsive information technologies."

—*Takahiro Fujimoto*
Professor, The University of Tokyo, Author, *The Evolution of a Manufacturing System at Toyota*, and Co-author (with Kim Clark), *Product Development Performance: Strategy, Organization, and Management in the World Auto Industry*

"Mukherjee captures very well the essential value that programs like PRM, Buy-Sell, and the internal knowledge management capabilities bring to HP every day."

—*Greg Shoemaker*
Vice President, Hewlett-Packard Company

"Once in a while I receive a book that makes me think 'Why did I not write this?' But of course, I could not. It takes a very experienced reflective practitioner, who in his heart is still an academic, to write such a wonderful book. I had the privilege to work with Mukherjee as a colleague at INSEAD almost 20 years ago.... I am truly pleased Mukherjee's ideas have finally found a place in a book."

—*Luk N. Van Wassenhove*
Henry Ford Chaired Professor of Manufacturing and Academic Director of the Social Innovation Center INSEAD

THE SPIDER'S STRATEGY

THE SPIDER'S STRATEGY

CREATING NETWORKS TO AVERT CRISIS, CREATE CHANGE, AND REALLY GET AHEAD

AMIT S. MUKHERJEE

For Connie —
Best wishes,
Amit
October 2008

Vice President, Publisher: Tim Moore
Associate Publisher and Director of Marketing: Amy Neidlinger
Acquisitions Editor: Martha Cooley
Editorial Assistant: Heather Luciano
Operations Manager: Gina Kanouse
Digital Marketing Manager: Julie Phifer
Publicity Manager: Laura Czaja
Assistant Marketing Manager: Megan Colvin
Marketing Assistant: Brandon Smith
Cover Designer: John Barnett
Managing Editor: Kristy Hart
Project Editor: Jovana San Nicolas-Shirley
Copy Editor: Gayle Johnson
Proofreader: Leslie Joseph
Indexer: Erika Millen
Senior Compositor: Jake McFarland
Manufacturing Buyer: Dan Uhrig

Published by Pearson Education, Inc.
Publishing as FT Press
Upper Saddle River, New Jersey 07458

FT Press offers excellent discounts on this book when ordered in quantity for bulk purchases
or special sales. For more information, please contact U.S. Corporate and Government Sales,
1-800-382-3419, corpsales@pearsontechgroup.com. For sales outside the U.S., please contact
International Sales at international@pearson.com.

Company and product names mentioned herein are the trademarks or registered trademarks
of their respective owners.

Printed in the United States of America

First Printing: August 2008

ISBN-10: 0-13-712665-4
ISBN-13: 978-0-13-712665-1

Pearson Education LTD.
Pearson Education Australia PTY, Limited.
Pearson Education Singapore, Pte. Ltd.
Pearson Education North Asia, Ltd.
Pearson Education Canada, Ltd.
Pearson Educatión de Mexico, S.A. de C.V.
Pearson Education—Japan
Pearson Education Malaysia, Pte. Ltd.

Library of Congress Cataloging-in-Publication Data

Mukherjee, Amit, 1958-
  The spider's strategy : creating networks to avert crisis, create change, and really get ahead /
Amit Mukherjee.
    p. cm.
  ISBN 0-13-712665-4 (hardback : alk. paper) 1. Business enterprises—Technological
innovations. 2. Technological innovations—Management. 3. Business networks.
4. Organizational change. I. Title.
  HD45.M846 2008
  658.5'14—dc22

                                                                          2008007912

For Sanghamitra Dutt, my wife
and
Michael Watkins, my friend

Contents

Part II: Design Principles for Adaptive Capabilities

                   The Importance of Being Earnestly Adaptive. 71

                   What Must the Company Sense?. 73

                   Four Operational Sense-and-Respond Systems 75

                        Nokia's Plan Reconfirmation Process 75

                        Yield Management with Sabre 77

                        Hewlett-Packard's Buy-Sell Process 78

                        Dell's Online Store 80

                   How to Design Sense-and-Respond Capabilities 81

                        Creating a Sensing Capability 82

                        Creating a Response Capability 83

                   The Role of Senior Executives. 86

                        Ensure That Multiple Sense-and-Respond
                        Capabilities Are Coherent 86

                        Determining the Role of Technology 87

                        Veering from Customer Intimacy to Being a
                        Peeping Tom 89

                        The Power to Reshape an Industry 91

Chapter 5:   Succeed in a Dog-Eat-Dog World 97

                   A Dog-Eat-Dog World. 100

                   Why Companies Act Against Their Own
                   Best Interests 102

                   The Importance of Playing Nice 105

                   Playing Nice—to Win. 107

                        The PRM Program at Hewlett-Packard 108

                        A Win-Win Policy at Nokia 111

                   Implementing the Second Design Principle 113

                        First, Recruit Passionate Believers 114

                        Focus on Solving Specific Practical Problems 116

                        Define Policies That Facilitate Information
                        Sharing 117

                        Change the Metrics 118

                        Recognize That It Takes Time to Overcome
                        Distrust 120

                   Nice Guys Aren't Finishing Last 121

Acknowledgments

New acquaintances often say, "I'm thinking of pursuing a doctor-ate. What would you suggest?" Every time, I reply with a question, "Are you a masochist?" I pause to enjoy the startled look on the person's face before continuing, "Because if you aren't, don't do it." I wish some author had thrown that response back at me the first time I said, "I'm thinking about writing a book on management." I suspect that if you hold a doctorate or are an author, you are ruefully chuck-ling about my observation right now!

I learned another lesson during the years I spent researching and writing this book: though the author's name goes on the cover, a book really cannot be written without the extreme kindness of friends, family, and strangers. Indeed, I've never even met two people who played a crucial role in making this book possible: Marianna Herold and Eero Eloranta, the two European academics who introduced me to Pertti Korhonen at Nokia. Incidentally, Professor Eloranta advised Nokia in the early years of its transformative efforts.

Pertti Korhonen generously contributed his time and perspec-tives on management and opened additional doors for me at Nokia. Jean-Francois Baril then met with and talked to me repeatedly. Both are amazingly passionate about the need for drastic change in the practice of management, and I really enjoyed spending time in their company. Tapio Markki provided a detailed look at how policy became practice at Nokia.

At Hewlett-Packard, Venu Nagali enthusiastically embraced the idea of this book. He not only shared his own experiences during repeated meetings, but he also got me access to his colleagues. His efforts—and those of Laura Wandke and Sarah Miller of Hill & Knowlton—enabled me to interview John Bowman, Karlheinz Hauber, Eric Schneider, and Patrick Scholler. The perspectives of these individuals gave me a deeper, more textured understanding of the challenges of managing transformational change.

I should, however, note here that the conclusions I reached about the actions and events at Nokia and Hewlett-Packard are my own; they are not official positions of either company.

SAP contributed valuable proprietary data about large businesses. Its former executive, Sudipta Bhattacharya, with whom I collaborated for several years on issues of strategy, challenged some of my ideas and so helped me sharpen them.

The Yankee Group let me use some of its data to make my case. Mike Conley, a former colleague who is an executive there, gave me access to its research.

Three business executives in whom I have profound trust—Phil Bennett, a consumer retailer; Sanghamitra Dutt, a banker; and Todd Rhodes, a technology consultant—gave me unvarnished feedback on my early drafts. They were not shy about telling me when I failed to hold their attention, and their input led me to reshape several chapters.

Takahiro Fujimoto, a professor at the University of Tokyo who is a former fellow doctoral candidate, provided valuable insight in his area of expertise, the worldwide automobile industry.

My friend Michael Watkins, an accomplished author, coached me through the process of getting the book written and published. Ike Williams, Hope Denekamp of Kneerim & Williams at Fish & Richardson, and Martha Cooley of Pearson arranged for publication by FT Press. I particularly appreciate Ike's and Martha's taking a risk on a first-time author.

Most of all, I am thankful to the many people who worked on the Nokia and Hewlett-Packard initiatives I have described, but whose contributions I have not discussed. It is impossible to tell coherent tales of organizational accomplishment without simplifying the many details.

❂   ❂   ❂

I would be remiss if I did not acknowledge here a person who cannot read these lines. Every reader of this book will soon be exposed to some of the ideas of Ramchandran Jaikumar, the former Daewoo Professor at the Harvard Business School. Jai, who was the chairman of my doctoral thesis committee, passed away prematurely in 1998. The word "genius" is overused, but Jai was undoubtedly one. I owe him considerable intellectual debt.

About the Author

Dr. Amit S. Mukherjee founded Ishan Advisors (http://www.ishanadvisors.com), an executive education and strategy consulting company, in 2004. He has worked as a consultant, line executive, and educator/researcher, and his diverse professional and life experiences have influenced this book.

He has worked closely with senior executives, including CEOs and Board members, of some of the world's best-known companies (SAP, Johnson & Johnson, Dunkin' Brands, Bekaert, Microsoft, Maytag, Bloomberg, and Sun), developing corporate and functional strategies. He has also led next-generation product-development efforts, managed key product-launch activities, negotiated intellectual property agreements, and worked on operational improvement projects with line workers on the graveyard shift.

Amit loves teaching, particularly at the executive level. He believes that business research should be empirical and practical. A major consulting company built a global practice based on his doctoral research, and two peer-reviewed papers he coauthored for a top management journal are extensively cited by others.

Prior to founding Ishan, as vice president and strategy advisor, Amit started Forrester Research's strategy consulting practice. He was the chief technology and strategy officer of TurboChef Technologies and a director (partner) at Arthur D. Little, where he served on two practice leadership teams. He was on the faculty of INSEAD and briefly, Georgetown's business school. He began his career at American Express Bank, after earning an MBA from the Darden School and a bachelor of engineering (with honors) from BITS (in India). Later, he earned his doctorate from the Harvard Business School.

Amit and his family live in Watertown, Massachusetts. He has also lived in India and France and has worked in several countries around the world. He speaks three languages, and in order to complete his doctoral thesis, he used a dictionary to temporarily gain sufficient understanding of a fourth. He enjoys hiking, cooking, traveling, and reading, and he still gets wistful about the days when he had time to enjoy cricket. He loves horses, especially Figaro, and one of these years, he plans to take up horseback riding.

Part I

Why Change?

"All great deeds and all great thoughts have a ridiculous beginning."

—Albert Camus, *The Myth of Sisyphus*

1

The Fire That Changed an Industry

About 8 p.m. on March 17, 2000, a lightning bolt struck a high-voltage electricity line in New Mexico. As power fluctuated across the state, a fire broke out in a fabrication line of the Royal Philips Electronics radio frequency chip manufacturing plant in Albuquerque.[1] Plant personnel reacted quickly and extinguished the fire within ten minutes. At first blush, it was clear that eight trays of silicon wafers on that line were destroyed. When fully processed, these would have produced chips for several thousand cell phones. A setback, no doubt, but definitely not a calamity.

At a chip factory, production takes place in "clean-room" conditions. The cleanest of such facilities have no more than one speck of dust per cubic foot. Stated differently, these facilities are ten thousand times cleaner than hospital operating rooms.[2] And therein lay the problem. Fire produces smoke and triggers sprinklers. Fire and smoke take lives, and sprinklers save them, but all—fire, smoke, and water—wreak havoc on property. As they dug deeper, plant personnel found that smoke and water had contaminated millions of chips that had been stored for shipment. Damage this extensive was definitely a calamity.

Four thousand miles away, at a Nokia plant outside Helsinki, a production planner who was following a well articulated process for managing chip inflows from Philips failed to get a routine input he needed from Philips. The failure could well have been an anomaly. Even so-called Six Sigma facilities (of which, despite the hype about the term, there are very few anywhere) produce 3.4 defects per million. Nevertheless, he informed the plant's purchasing manager, and again following an established process, they passed on word of a possible problem to Tapio Markki, the top component purchasing manager.

In Albuquerque, Philips engineers and managers grappled with the aftermath of the fire. They realized that cleanup would take at least a week, which meant that customers would be affected, at least temporarily. Nokia and its archrival, Ericsson, accounted for 40% of the plant's shipments. Philips management decided that their orders would be filled first when the plant returned to normal.

On March 20, Philips called its customers, including Mr. Markki. He recalls that Philips said that the disruption would last about a week. The *Wall Street Journal* article (cited earlier and published months later) implied that Philips had underestimated the extent of the problem.

Mr. Markki had, early in his career, worked for five years at a small semiconductor company that supplied Nokia. He told me, "I knew the cleanup would take more than one week (but) for me it wasn't special." Nevertheless, in a culture that encouraged discussing possible problems openly, he informed his bosses, including Pertti Korhonen, then Senior Vice President of Operations, Logistics, and Sourcing for Nokia Mobile Phones. Nokia's production planner began checking the status of the five parts made in New Mexico once a day instead of the customary once a week. Nokia had developed this enhanced monitoring process over the prior five years. Several components—almost all from normally functioning plants—received the same treatment each year if Nokia became concerned with their maker's performance for any reason.

A few hundred miles away, executives at Ericsson also got a call from Philips. Until this call, Ericsson's planners and managers had not sensed any discrepancy in Philips' performance. As such, its management had no reason to disbelieve Philips' explanations. They certainly did not perceive a need for concern or stepped-up action.

Nokia's intensified tracking and communications with Philips did not raise Nokia's confidence that its partner had the problem under control. Its executives began regularly urging their counterparts at Philips to take stronger action. They also moved toward adopting the response routines they had developed for such eventualities. On March 31, exactly two weeks after the fire, Philips admitted it would need more time to fix the problem; ultimately, the plant remained out of action for six weeks.

Recognizing that Philips' problem could affect the production of several million mobile phones, Nokia took three key steps:

- One team of executives and engineers focused on Philips, seeking a major role in developing alternative plans. Guided by Mr. Korhonen and assisted by CEO Jorma Ollila, it pressed Nokia's case with Philips executives, including its CEO, Cor Boonstra. Philips responded by rearranging its plans in factories as far away as Eindhoven and Shanghai.
- A second cross-continental team redesigned some chips so that they could be produced in other Philips and non-Philips plants. Where appropriate, it consulted with Philips to assess the possible impact of its actions.
- A third group worked to find alternative manufacturers to reduce pressure on Philips. Two current suppliers responded within five days.

The magnitude of the cooperation between Nokia and Philips cannot be fully appreciated without a few words on Philips. Once considered a leading-edge technology company, by the mid-1990s Philips was being criticized by many an analyst. Mr. Boonstra ignored their calls to dismember the company and instead spent three years reshaping it and rebuilding its reputation. In 2000, Philips' Semiconductor Division was functioning very well.[3] It had acquired several plants from IBM and boosted its production capacity 40% over 1999 levels.

Its seventeen plants were churning out eighty million chips a day; these chips were used in 80% of the mobile phones sold worldwide. That year, chip volume grew 33% and revenues 55%. Despite the fire—which did not merit a single sentence in Philips' 2000 annual report—divisional operating income rose 119%.[4] This superb performance meant that Philips simply had no surplus capacity. Helping Nokia required managerial and technical effort equivalent to pulling a rabbit out of a hat.

Philips' predicament was not unique. In 2000, the mobile phone market was growing at over 40% per annum, but so were the markets for laptops and other electronics. Component makers, ranging from chip to liquid crystal display producers, were working at capacity.[5] Some consumer electronics companies were ready to pay virtually any price for key components. By midyear, Sony, Micron Technology, Dell, Sun, and even Philips itself had announced that component shortages would rein in their (very strong) financial performances. Shortages were expected to continue unabated till year-end.

At the end of March, in this market environment, Ericsson finally came to appreciate the gravity of its problem. However, for reasons about which one can only speculate, it still did not act speedily. Jan Warby, the executive who headed the mobile phone division, did not get involved till early April. By then Ericsson had very few options left.

Nokia's initial sensing of the problem and its rapid and effective response carried the day. In the third quarter of 2000, its profits rose 42% as it expanded its share of the global market to 30%. *Its quarterly statements and annual report for 2000 did not even mention the fire.*

On July 20, 2000, Ericsson reported that the fire and component shortages had caused a second-quarter operating loss of $200 million in its mobile phone division. As such, annual earnings would be lower by between $333 million and $445 million.[6] Six months later, it reported divisional annual losses of $1.68 billion, a 3% loss of market share, and corporate operating losses of $167 million. It also announced the outsourcing of cell phone manufacturing to Flextronics and the elimination of several thousand jobs; Flextronics took over Ericsson's plants in Brazil, Malaysia, Sweden, the U.K., and the U.S. In April 2001, it signed a Memorandum of Understanding to create Sony Ericsson; the informal negotiations that led to this step had started at the height of the crisis in July 2000, though Ericsson had denied it in public. The deal was finalized in October 2001.

Ericsson's woes spread beyond mobile phones and continued into subsequent years. It finally returned to health in 2004, but as a much smaller company. Compared to 2000, its revenues had fallen 52%, total assets about 30%, and number of employees 52%; net income and operating income were almost, but not quite, the same.

The face of the mobile phone industry had changed forever, all because of a fire that had been contained in ten minutes.

That was an exciting story, but so what?

Since early 2001, stories about the fire have appeared in many publications and forums. Some—but only a fraction—of the articles that have appeared are listed in the endnotes of this and subsequent chapters. Collectively, these stories perpetuated several myths:

- **Myth #1: Nokia succeeded because it relied on individual effort, while Ericsson relied on teams.**   No individual—or even a group of individuals acting independently—could have pulled off the cross-continental, cross-organizational response that Nokia took. When I interviewed him at the Nokia headquarters at Espoo, Finland, in the spring of 2006, Mr. Korhonen made it clear that Nokia's culture did not tolerate individualistic cowboys.

- **Myth #2: Nokia succeeded because it used superior information technology.**   Several software makers claimed that their software had helped Nokia, and some technology analysts wrote that IT had saved it from Ericsson's fate. Like most large companies, Nokia could not have functioned without IT. However, IT played a supporting role, and the specific benefit it gave Nokia was so prosaic that no technology partisan that I know ever wrote about it.

- **Myth #3: Nokia succeeded because Finns are less cautious than Swedes.** An explanation rooted in unfounded national stereotypes has little to teach us and is undoubtedly wrong. In any case, *national* culture played no role; a French executive, Jean-Francois Baril, who had spent many years in the U.S., led the building of many of Nokia's capabilities.

- **Myth #4: Nokia succeeded because Mr. Korhonen was a brilliant crisis manager.** Mr. Korhonen and Nokia replaced James Burke and Johnson & Johnson's handling of the Tylenol cyanide poisoning as the poster child for impeccable crisis management. Academics use the story to illustrate types of crises that companies must be able to withstand and to cajole them to upgrade their supply chains. Risk management professionals use it to scare potential clients into buying appropriate insurance. In reality—and despite the fact that the *Wall Street Journal* article quoted Mr. Korhonen as calling the situation a "crisis"—*Nokia successfully avoided the crisis that engulfed Ericsson.* A long way into our conversation, perhaps after he felt that I understood what Nokia had really done, Mr. Korhonen said:

  > Externally, the fire has been a much bigger thing than internally. For us, it has been business as usual. We have had to manage many such things.

Mr. Korhonen did play a key role—but mostly during the prior five years, when Nokia created the capabilities that enabled it to shrug off a challenge that has captivated the business world. These capabilities—built into its strategy, processes, and values and supported by technology—enabled it to *adapt* rapidly to huge changes in the assumptions embedded in its business plans. Even today, seven years after the fire and almost eleven years after Nokia began transforming itself, only a handful of large companies can do what Nokia did in 2000.

Such a capability is exceedingly important, because we live in a *networked* world in which each company partners with a set of other companies. A company's network extends from its customer-facing side, through its product and technology development functions, and on to its supply network side. While such networks are critical to modern businesses, they enable shifts in market or operating conditions to rapidly propagate far beyond their origins. If a company is unable to sense such a shift and respond effectively, it can lose tremendous amounts of value, see the reputations of its senior executives tarnished, and destroy the livelihoods of thousands.

Companies—like Nokia—that can intelligently and effortlessly adjust to major shifts in market or operating conditions are Adaptive Businesses.

Design Principles for Adaptive Businesses

This book presents four Design Principles that senior executives can apply to transform their companies into businesses that will thrive in a networked world. A Design Principle is a guideline for policy, rather than a template to stamp out identical sets of tools and procedures. Indeed, I do not believe it is possible to provide replicable templates; companies must use the Principles to create their own unique solutions. The Principles are as follows:

1. *Embed sense-and-respond capabilities within normal plan-and-execute processes.* The ability to detect a problem (or opportunity) early and correctly and the ability to react effectively are key determinants of competitive advantage. Unless these abilities are a part of everyday work, companies will lurch from crisis to crisis, be they big or small.

2. *Adopt strategies that promote collaborative action among network partners.* As they globalize and as their supply-and-demand networks fracture, companies lose visibility into aspects of their competitive landscape. Unless they develop cooperative relationships with their partners, they will not get preferential assistance with either crisis or opportunity.

3. ***Value and nurture organizational learning.*** Companies must collect, analyze, and share across their networks knowledge about what works and what does not. Absent such "intelligent knowledge sharing," they will lack information to act decisively and effectively.

4. ***Deploy technologies that enable intelligent adjustment to major environmental shifts.*** To adjust to changed conditions effectively and efficiently, companies must apply information technologies that support the prior principles.

The four Principles are deceptively simple; stating them is far easier than applying them day after day. For example, despite embarking on its transformation in 1995, Nokia has only recently become comfortable with the idea that its adaptive capabilities are inextricably interwoven into the fabric of its organization. Hewlett-Packard—another company that I will profile extensively—also began changing at the same time and is still institutionalizing the capabilities it has built.

The difficulty of implementing the Principles is what gives them their great power; *collectively they change how work is performed on a day-to-day basis*. For example, to sense and respond, one might need the preferential help of a partner company. This presumes that the companies look after each other's interests. Technology aids the ability to sense and respond, but unless people can make sense of what they are sensing, all the effort will be for naught.

Companies also must consider major organizational changes in order to marshal and deploy people with the skills needed to design, create, and manage their networks. Many may decide to centralize these people in a coherent group, while others may decide to keep them dispersed but well linked. In either case, they must consider appointing a senior executive to give them a voice in top management deliberations. Whether or not he or she actually holds the title formally, this executive, the Chief Network Officer, will bear primary responsibility for the four Design Principles. No company that I know of, including Nokia, currently uses this title; nevertheless, a couple of key people at Nokia have played the Chief Network Officer's *role* well.

Seen through the lenses of Adaptive Businesses and network management, Nokia and Philips treated each other as *preferential* partners and won. Ericsson, which had no one to "watch its back" when the chips were down (literally and figuratively!), lost. Ironically, the lesson Ericsson took away was not one of codependence; instead, it resolved never again to become dependent on a single supplier.

Organization of the Book

In the rest of Part I, "Why Change?," I build the case for transforming the modern enterprise by addressing its key limitations and the impact they have on performance.

Chapter 2, "Shadows of the Past," first summarizes a fascinating piece of historical research that tracks how and why companies have changed over the last two-hundred-odd years. In response to periodic "epochal" shifts, companies have modified how work is performed, how their organizations are structured, and even their corporate ethos. Distributed computer networks are driving the present epochal change by fragmenting work across time and space, engendering extreme product customization, and blurring industrial boundaries. In this environment, companies will fall into *the execution trap* if they believe that reliance on traditional "good management"—plan well and execute brilliantly—*alone* will help them succeed.

Chapter 3, "Visions from the Present," advances the case for corporate transformation. In order to succeed in a world of corporate networks, companies must develop three capabilities to augment their traditional plan-and-execute skills. They must be able to sense changes in their environments, respond to these seamlessly, and learn from their experiences and apply the lessons in other situations.

Senior executives should take responsibility for guiding this transformation, because research shows that financial markets are penalizing companies and executives for perceived failures more severely than ever before.

Part II, "Design Principles for Adaptive Capabilities," lays out the four Design Principles that can transform a company.

Chapter 4, "Transform Everyday Work," introduces the first Design Principle: **Embed sense-and-respond capabilities within normal plan-and-execute processes.** Without embedding, a company cannot be adaptive; at best, it can be great at managing crises. Embedding requires changing work practices, just as becoming truly quality-focused requires making quality the responsibility of individual employees.

Chapter 5, "Succeed in a Dog-Eat-Dog World," explains the second Design Principle: **Adopt strategies that promote collaborative action among network partners.** The fragmentation of work will require companies to create win-win partnerships with their partners, because no company can succeed while its network is ailing. Research shows that executives recognize the need for collaboration, but this does not always lead to action. Understanding why companies act against their best interests can help executives change such behavior.

Chapter 6, "Ensure That Work Teaches," discusses the third Design Principle: **Value and nurture organizational learning.** The failure to learn keeps companies from intelligent and effortless adaptation. It impedes both the effective use of the prior Principles and the interpretation of environmental signals to take action. Executives must understand how they can manage culture, systems, and organizational structure to improve their companies' ability to learn.

Chapter 7, "Make Technology Matter," provides focused guidance on the fourth Design Principle: **Deploy technologies that enable intelligent adjustment to major environmental shifts.** It asserts that companies must invest in technologies that *provide visibility, support analysis, facilitate collaboration,* or *enable mobility.* Technologies that do not build these capabilities may be essential for security or legal reasons, but they will not provide competitive advantage. This discussion focuses on technology strategy (what, why) and not technical details (how).

Part III, "Going Adaptive," discusses the challenging task of transforming a company into an Adaptive Business by systematically implementing the four Design Principles.

Chapter 8, "Create the Organization," addresses the organizational changes companies must make. Managing internal and external networks must become a focal point for key decisions. People who are superb at designing, creating, and managing human networks will undertake this task and increasingly become highly prized by their employers. A Chief Network Officer, who may or may not be formally designated as such, should lead them.

Chapter 9, "Introduce Change Holographically," deals with the general management challenge of initiating the transformation and maintaining momentum. Companies must adopt what I call *holographic change management*. This approach advocates the implementation of all four Design Principles in one business area and subsequent replication in other areas. It also advises against implementing one Design Principle at a time across the entire company.

The Epilogue brings closure by describing two perspectives on an Adaptive Business. One comes from a junior manager who works at the company, while the other comes from this person's CEO.

Given my focus on *corporate* transformation, many of the issues I discuss fall within the bailiwicks of top managers. Starting with Chapter 2, I make specific recommendations for them. However, becoming adaptive is not a spectator sport for middle managers and other professionals; indeed, Hewlett-Packard's efforts have been led by such people. Most chapters, therefore, end with a sidebar titled "So You Are Not the CEO...," which addresses the critical roles these professionals must play.

Basis of the Ideas

Historically, most "big ideas" in management arose in the manufacturing sector and then spread to the service sector. Adaptive Businesses, too, are evolving in manufacturing (and retail) companies, but will sooner or later migrate to the service businesses. (Indeed, a top strategy executive of a major British manufacturer recently argued coherently that a premier American investment bank applies all four of the Design Principles and is no less adaptive than Nokia.)

So, this book builds on a robust intellectual foundation of research on manufacturers. I also present evidence from a study of over five hundred manufacturing and retail companies that I conducted a few years ago for the software firm SAP. I supplement these with stories, some from the media, but many others from over a quarter century of personal association with companies in industries that include steel wire, food, white goods, glass, medical devices, pharmaceuticals, consumer-packaged goods, and electronics. I have advised several CEOs—and other C-level executives—of global firms, led cross-organizational product-development efforts, and worked on the graveyard shift beside line workers carping about managerial idiocies. I protect their confidentiality by not naming them, but I do provide enough contextual information to make the stories meaningful.

Most importantly, I draw on many hours of interviews (and associated secondary research) that I have conducted at Nokia and Hewlett-Packard. To the best of my knowledge, Nokia has not given anyone else similar access to the executives involved. These two stories—Nokia's in particular—present a comprehensive picture of the transformation that companies must undergo. I cannot credibly call for *multidimensional* change and then provide piecemeal examples cobbled together from different firms facing divergent challenges. For the record, neither company is—or has been—a client of mine. What they have created, they have done on their own.

Endnotes

[1] I have pieced together the description of the fire and, indeed, the broader story of what happened at Nokia, Ericsson, and Philips from interviews I conducted, numerous news reports, website descriptions of technology companies, and annual reports. Of the news reports, the best known is "Trial by Fire: A Blaze in Albuquerque Sets off Major Crisis for Cell-Phone Giants. Nokia Handles Supply Shock with Aplomb as Ericsson of Sweden Gets Burned—Was Sisu the Difference?" by Almar Latour, the *Wall Street Journal*, January 29, 2001. Other newspaper and newsmagazine citations are given here and in subsequent chapters in conjunction with specific quotes.

[2] Intel website, http://www.intel.com/education/cleanroom/index2.htm.

[3] Royal Philips Electronics annual report for 2000 (pp. 38–39 and 60–61).

[4] A single line in the 2001 report noted an insurance payoff for damages sustained due to the fire.

[5] "Companies fear no end in sight for component shortages," by Rachel Konrad, CNET News.com, July 26, 2000.

[6] "Ericsson's Mobile Worries," BBC, July 21, 2000, 21:35 GMT, 22:35 UK, http://news.bbc.co.uk/2/hi/business/845619.stm.

2

Shadows of the Past

I will begin building the case for Adaptive Businesses with a walk through the history of manufacturing companies. Ramchandran Jaikumar—or Jai, as he was widely known—a brilliant mind who once occupied the Daewoo Chair at the Harvard Business School, will guide us.[1] Jai won the Frederick Winslow Taylor Medal, advised the U.S. Congress, and guided executive officers and the Boards of several top global companies. One of these companies was the Italian gun maker Beretta, which has been controlled by the same family for five hundred years. Beretta gave Jai access to the meticulous records it maintained over the centuries of all the changes it had experienced.[2]

By the end of the 1980s, Beretta had gone through several major paradigm shifts (see Table 2-1) that Jai called "epochs." Each started with the introduction of a new, often deceptively simple technology. Yet, over a period of ten years in the best-managed companies and about fifty years in most others, each epoch changed virtually everything of importance and wreaked havoc on people, companies, and even societies. What was most apparent were huge (measured in the hundreds of percents) increases in productivity and quality. Less visible were the real drivers of these improvements: the complete transformation of the systems and nature of work, skills required of people, and organizational structures.

For example, between 1500 and 1800, "manufacturing" did not exist; people made things. To get the right to make a gun in Europe, a young man had to apprentice with a master gun maker, a member of

TABLE 2-1   Jal's Epochs of Manufacturing, Showing How the Very Structure of Business Changed

Epochs		Performance Changes				Number of People / % Staff	Managerial Changes		
Period	Name	Technological Drivers	Productivity Rise Over the Past	Percent Rework	Number of Products		Changes in Organization Structure	How Work Is Transformed	Ethos: What Is Valued
Before 1800	Make, not manufacture				1			Master inspects	Artisan skills
1789–1800	English System	Flat plane, micrometer, engineering drawings	400%	80%	No limit	40 / 0%	Guilds break up	Worker inspects	Accuracy in mechanical craft
1798–1855	American System	Specialized machines, go/no-go gauges	300%	50%	3	150 / 13%	Quality control, use of outside contractors	Foremen supervise work tightly	Precision in repetitive work
1890–1920	Scientific Management	Stopwatch, job studies, empirical data	300%	25%	10	300 / 20%	Jobs specialized by function	Foremen supervise work lightly and problems closely	Decompose and deskill work
1930s–1960	Dynamic Control	SPC charts, semiautomated machines	150%	8%	15	300 / 33%	Problem solving teams formed	Workers assess problems, supervisors lightly review	Diagnose problems

TABLE 2-1   Jai's Epochs of Manufacturing, Showing How the Very Structure of Business Changed

Epochs			Performance Changes			Managerial Changes			
Period	Name	Technological Drivers	Productivity Rise Over the Past	Percent Rework	Number of Products	Number of People / % Staff	Changes in Organization Structure	How Work Is Transformed	Ethos: What Is Valued
1940s–1970	Numeric Control	Microprocessors and automatic tool changing	300%	2%	100	100 / 50%	Multiple functions integrated	Limited or no supervision	Experiment to improve
1970–?	Computer-Integrated Manufacturing	CAD, CAM, and FMS	300%	0.5%	No limit	30 / 67%	R&D and plants integrated	Limited or no supervision	Learn and generalize

Adapted from *From Filing and Fitting to Flexible Manufacturing*
CAD: Computer-Aided Design
CAM: Computer-Aided Manufacturing
FMS: Flexible Manufacturing System

a powerful guild. Each gun was individually handcrafted, and the sun rose and set with the word of the master; he alone had the authority to pronounce work acceptable.

In 1789, Henry Maudslay, considered the father of the modern machine tool industry, initiated the first epochal change, the "English System." He introduced two simple tools to his workshop in the Woolwich Arsenal. The first was a precise micrometer nicknamed the "Lord Chancellor," and the second, a flat surface, was called a "standard plane." These tools, augmented by Gaspard Mogne's concept of engineering drawings, enabled workers *for the first time* to accurately measure the dimensions of the products they had to build.

Beretta adopted these ideas in 1810. Quality improved so much that in contrast to traditional work practices, every product did *not* require rework. This raised productivity 400%. But far more importantly—and unexpectedly—no longer did the master have to put his personal stamp of approval on each product; each worker could inspect his own work and decide whether it was satisfactory.

This fact transformed Beretta. The number of workers in a workshop rose from eight to forty. The organization within the workshops had hitherto been based on craftsmen's guilds; this was no longer necessary. The Beretta family no longer had to hire great masters and trust them to bring in their own apprentices; they could directly hire and train young people. Moreover, people who, for hundreds of years, had filed and fitted together small pieces of metal after machining them roughly on lathes could now focus on accurately machining the work pieces on their lathes. A different set of skills and a different knowledge base became critical.

Like the Woolrich Arsenal and Beretta, workshops that gave workers access to micrometers and standard planes, instead of limiting them to the masters, began producing better-quality products. This inevitably meant that workshops that did not take these steps could not compete. Since Darwin's ideas about survival of the fittest do not just apply to biological systems, *over time, these simple tools trans-formed how most companies worked.*

Consequently, outside the factory, a huge societal shift occurred. No longer did young men who wanted a profession making products have to apprentice themselves to masters for many years. They did not even have to aspire to become gun makers; they could make anything that could be made with a lathe, a plane surface, and a micrometer. Over time, the guild system collapsed. The first paradigm shift, the "English System," had transformed the nature of the company, the task of management, and, indeed, the Western world.

More than 150 years later, the fourth of Jai's epochs took shape. Another simple tool, the statistical process control (SPC) chart, again enabled a very sharp leap forward in quality and a bigger leap in productivity. Developed in the U.S., this tool found its true home in Japan. Augmented by Taiichi Ohno's Just-in-Time, it transformed companies yet again.

In companies that adopted SPC, the nature of work changed again. Compared to the prior era (Scientific Management, introduced by Fredrick Winslow Taylor), the responsibility for solving problems returned to the worker, *but not to individual workers.* Problem-solving teams, typically cross-functional, began to flourish. The key skill required of people was no longer working accurately, but being able to diagnose and solve problems when they occurred. This meant that the level of education and training needed to perform basic jobs rose.

As with every other epoch, companies that made the appropriate changes thrived. This certainly happened in Japan. A once devastated country known for creating shoddy products became the beacon for quality and transformed itself into the world's second most powerful economy. For example, in the air conditioning equipment industry, the Japanese company with the worst performance produced products of an order of magnitude better quality than the American company with the best performance.[3] Conversely, companies foundered if they did not provide people with the knowledge to apply SPC and did not change the nature of the work so that their workers, not foremen and managers, could make most decisions. In the U.S., for example, performance differences such as those in the air conditioning equipment industry produced large-scale economic dislocation.

In the early years of the twenty-first century, while we are well beyond the fourth epoch, we lack the objectivity that arises from the distance of time to truly assess where we stand. Are we in the throes of Jai's last epoch—Computer-Integrated Manufacturing (CIM)? Or has Jai's sixth epoch been superseded by one based on Internet-based technologies? My views are based on applying Jai's ideas—and the related research that I did—in manufacturers around the world: Jai was simultaneously premature and prescient in defining CIM as the sixth epoch.

Jai was premature because CIM did spring up, as is often the case with new technologies, in the weapons industry. Some companies outside this industry, mostly machine tool makers in Japan, also made the transition.[4] However, these beachheads did not lead to broadscale change. I believe that the single most important reason for this failure was the lack of computing power. Through the 1980s and half of the 1990s, few companies had computing power that was available on demand to "integrate" all work throughout their organizations. Consequently, the epoch that Jai described as CIM has turned out merely to be an extension of the *fifth* epoch, Numerically Controlled Machines, which relied heavily on *local* computational power.

Jai was prescient because starting in the late 1990s, computers could appear on many more desktops because they had become enormously more powerful and much cheaper. They could also be linked, both within companies and over the Internet with computers in other companies. Individually, these machines could do wonders; collectively, a group of them could outperform many a supercomputer. I believe that this change brought the business world to its sixth epochal change, one driven by *distributed computer networks*. It is at this point that the power Jai had envisioned for the CIM epoch truly emerged.

As I will discuss next, Ericsson's experiences before and after the fire illustrate how distributed computer networks changed the business landscape on a scale that rivals the emergence of the prior epochs. This epoch, however, has one characteristic that the prior ones did not: it has already extended itself beyond the boundaries of manufacturers, tying them very closely to retail businesses. In recognition of this fact, I use the term "Adaptive Business"—rather than a term more consistent with Jai's choice of names—to describe this epoch.

"Toto, I've a Feeling We're Not in Kansas Anymore"

Much of the 1990s had been exceptionally good for Ericsson. Under CEO Lars Ramqvist, it grew very rapidly. As such, market capitalization rose 40% annually between 1991 and 1997 and 58% annually between 1995 and 1997. In January 1998, Ericsson appointed Mr. Ramqvist chairman and promoted Sven-Christer Nilsson, the erstwhile head of the U.S. phone systems business, to president and CEO. Mr. Nilsson bested a slate of twenty executives considered for the job.

Mr. Nilsson spent his first three months as CEO visiting Ericsson offices worldwide. In L. Frank Baum's *The Wizard of Oz*, the protagonist, Dorothy, discovers that a tornado has magically removed her from her simple homeland and deposited her in the Land of the Munchkins. She tells her dog, "Toto, I've a feeling we're not in Kansas anymore." Quite possibly, Mr. Nilsson's travels left him feeling the same: Ericsson was being buffeted by three megatrends that accompanied the new epoch and these were changing the landscape of modern business.

The Decomposition of Work

The first major trend accompanying the new epoch was the decomposition of work across time and space. It began with the emergence of global data communication capabilities. In contrast to the communication of voice, this decomposition caused companies to extend their creation of intellectual property to locations around the world. Engineers in Europe and America could now use software to view and analyze 3D renderings of new products created by their compatriots in Asia. In fact, they could see how the parts would actually work together if and when they were built. This gave companies the confidence to break up work across networks of temporally and geographically dispersed—and often financially independent—workgroups.

Though information technology outsourcing has captured the public's imagination, today, companies as different as Boeing, Proctor & Gamble, and Hewlett-Packard are outsourcing larger chunks of work. A *Business Week* article on the subject repeatedly returned to Flextronics, the huge provider of outsourced design and manufacturing services. Flextronics has acquired frog, the design powerhouse that helped Apple create the first Macintosh.[5] It intends to offer design and manufacturing services from around the globe:

> Inside frog's hip Sunnyvale office, designers are working to create a radically new multimedia device.... The plan, says Patricia Roller, frog's co-CEO, is to use Flextronics software engineers in Ukraine or India to develop innovative applications, and for Flextronics engineers to design the working prototype. Flextronics then would mass-produce the gadgets, probably in China.

But work decomposition is not simply restricted to large companies. In the late 1990s, as the Chief Technology & Strategy Officer of a small public high-technology company, I directed the development of a next-generation user interface for a residential product. My engineers in Dallas, Texas, designed a prototype system held together by the proverbial baling wire and sealing wax. I then contracted with LG

Soft (India), the software and embedded systems design arm of the Korean giant LG Electronics, to design the product in Bangalore, India. We agreed that LG Electronics' Korean laboratories would give the design physical form and that LG Electronics' plants in North and South America would mass-produce it.[6]

Such decomposition of work was inconceivable even two decades ago. Companies often ran their overseas units as outposts that simply imported products or exported raw materials. Some operated them even more independently, simply passing monies to and from the parent country. The pace of growth of these outposts and how they operated had little impact on the parents' overall functioning or health. Even where operating links transcended boundaries of countries, the connections were well buffered.[7] In contrast, today, few foreign operations, if any, are anywhere nearly as isolated. Raw material, finished goods, work-in-process, monies, and information flow fast and furious from R&D centers located in one country to suppliers in another to manufacturing plants in a third to sales offices in a fourth.

In the 1990s, Ericsson was also feeling the power of this trend. By 1996, 117 countries had bought and installed its premier telecommunications infrastructure product line (AXE). In 1999, Ericsson had a market (sales) presence in an astounding 140 countries and expanded its distribution network. It had 38 active production facilities in 15 countries. That year, it started a new plant in Malaysia and a second joint venture facility in China, while expanding production in Brazil. It outsourced enough production to partners to warrant a comment in its annual report and also sold two plants to its partners.

What Have You Done for Me Lately?

The second major epochal trend is an explosion in the variety of output being produced by companies. Distributed computer networks make possible outputs whose variety far exceeds the ability of most companies to effectively manage the variety.

When Toyota brought Lean Enterprise into the U.S. in the early 1980s, U.S. car dealers routinely offered customers a price quote and an expected delivery date—typically two to three months out—for cars with the exact features they wanted. Toyota did not; it offered customers only preconfigured "value packages." Even so, customers came to prefer the benefits—higher quality, lower price, and immediate delivery—of Toyota's approach. Their conversion not only brought U.S. automakers to their knees, but also changed the industry's standard practice. Many young people today do not even know that customized cars were not unusual in the past.

In contrast, they do know that Dell sells a virtually infinite variation of its computer line profitably. Dell's strategy has allowed it to run one of the leanest enterprises around. It arguably forced IBM, which typically had a better, but more expensive, product, to exit the laptop personal computer market and contributed to Carly Fiorina's loss of the CEO position at Hewlett-Packard. In doing so, it seemingly validated the virtues of offering customers what they wanted instead of giving them what the company wanted to sell (however, see Chapter 4, "Transform Everyday Work").

The twenty-five years that elapsed between these two stories introduced two major changes. First, today most products and the processes that create them have microprocessors and software embedded in them. This makes some degree of customization easy, at least from a technical perspective. The fact that something is customizable then gives sellers the incentive to promote customization and buyers the incentive to demand it. Second, customization is valued only if the time to delivery is short and the incremental cost is minimal. This means that sellers must have superbly managed supply-and-demand networks to keep buyers happy.

Given Dell's financial successes, it is not surprising that for much of the last decade, most companies with branded products have tried to emulate its aggressive customization strategy. In the survey of

North American businesses I conducted for SAP, my team of MBAs and engineers interviewed general managers of business units and executives and managers from manufacturing, engineering, logistics, and information technology. The interviewees came from over four hundred firms from the North American automobile, pharmaceutical, chemical, consumer packaged goods (CPG), and high-technology industries and over one hundred retail companies. They worked for business units whose sales ranged from $500 million to over $10 billion. Almost all used modern management techniques like Lean and information technology tools like Enterprise Resource Planning (ERP). The survey found a very strong commitment to variety and customization:[8]

- 25% of the respondents reported selling more than *five thousand* distinct end products.
- 65% of the business unit general managers reported feeling "more or much more" pressure than in the past to introduce product variants.
- 75% of them reported feeling similar pressure to get new products to market faster.
- Well over 60% of the companies reported producing more product variants than they had two years earlier.

In Ericsson's case, the global market seemingly had an insatiable appetite for new models. In the high-end Japanese market, the most demanding in the world, young, computer-savvy consumers voraciously demanded ever fancier features and accessories. At the other extreme, the low-priced segment accounted for most of the simple units sold worldwide. The "professional segment" in the middle, consisting of business and industrial buyers, needed phones that could withstand water, dust, and shocks. Ericsson felt it could not ignore any segment. The cutting-edge demands of the Japanese market inevitably trickled down to the other segments, while the low-end segment, despite its low profit margins, provided the sheer numbers it needed to lead the industry. So, in 1997 and 1998, Ericsson introduced thirty new cell phones. To fend off price pressures from a stream of new entrants, particularly those from China, it also made a concerted effort to establish a discernable brand name worldwide.

Simultaneously, Ericsson had to navigate the rapid and uncertain change affecting the industry's basic technology platforms. GSM, TDMA, and CDMA platforms were selling side by side; these constituted the so-called 2G (second-generation) phones. 3G, which could truly exploit the power of the Internet, seemed close and yet so far; it was increasingly becoming clear that a "2.5G" would be needed to pave the way. The different markets across the world were embracing the technologies at different paces. The U.S., for example, seemed to show no inclination toward moving off the TDMA and CDMA platforms prevalent there.

The Blurring of Industries

The third major trend accompanying the epochal change is one half of a tug-of-war over the basic structure of industries. One side of this war has received considerable attention: many industries that exist today did not in the past. In the U.S., this fact has led to the replacement of the venerable Standard Industrial Codes (SIC) system for categorizing industries with the more flexible North American Industry Classification System (NAICS). The other side of this war has not received as much attention, despite being just as important and powerful: the traditional demarcations between industries are increasingly blurring and are sometimes getting erased. For example:

- Some parts of the consumer packaged goods industry are hard to distinguish from parts of the pharmaceutical industry and, indeed, parts of the chemical industry. Indeed, the chemical industry is also a key supplier to both the CPG and pharmaceutical industries.

- In the auto industry, in contrast to fairly recent history, electronics account for a significant proportion of the cost of a premier car. Automakers now have to work with an industry whose fortunes did not concern them a few years ago. Yet, long-time suppliers of sheet metal, transmissions, glass, leather, and foam have not gone away. In fact, some of the electronics now have to be embedded in—or at least connected to—many of these standard components.

- In healthcare, lifesaving devices like cardiac stents now come coated with drugs that improve their efficacy, in effect merging the hitherto distinct pharmaceutical and medical device industries. The rising stature of biotechnology will further complicate matters. The embryonic nanotechnology industry already has signaled its ambitions by developing microdevices that can cut, clean, and repair within our bodies.

Distributed computer networks not only make it easy to imagine how industries could converge, but also make their linkage possible quickly and easily. In Ericsson's case, two major convergences occurred virtually simultaneously. First, the basic business in telecommunications infrastructure not only could, but had to, become capable of supporting mobile phones. In its 1999 annual report, Ericsson discussed the symbiotic relationship emerging between these businesses:

> The demand for various types of mobile data services also brings a strongly increased need for capacity in the mobile networks, resulting in demand for new infrastructure investments by operators. To take full advantage of the new technology, subscribers will require new and advanced mobile terminals—terminals that are currently being developed by Ericsson.[9]

Second, the telecommunications industry and the Internet began converging. Ericsson had to begin wrestling with the seemingly explosive demands of providing telecommunications services directly to consumers' homes. If it did not, it could not only lose the opportunity to pursue potentially huge revenues, but could also possibly lose control over rapidly changing technologies that were clearly forcing these businesses together.

The Execution Trap

Over the last fifty years, leading thinkers and top practitioners of management have worshipped at the altar of good planning and flawless execution. This worship is observable about two-thirds or three-fourths of the way through each fiscal year, when companies start developing financial plans for the next year. These then get translated into specific tasks for which people can be "held accountable" during monthly, quarterly, and annual performance reviews. Do plan and execute well—especially the latter—and you will be anointed a great manager. Fail at either—especially the latter—and regardless of the cause, you will be considered a loser who does not deserve the accoutrements of high office.

However, Jai's research taught a harsh lesson: *doctrines of good management that work beautifully in one epoch tend to be inadequate in the next*. In the Adaptive Business epoch, *simply* planning well and executing brilliantly will no longer guarantee great results. Any company that fails to appreciate this fact will find itself well cocooned in the breast of the Execution Trap: the company will focus ever harder on brilliant execution but still will not be able to substantially improve performance.

The Execution Trap is a direct consequence of the collective action of the three trends. They make work too complex to meticulously plan and flawlessly execute in accordance with the plan. Individually and collectively, they limit managers' visibility into their vast empires. Plans developed, often with the help of powerful computers, are unable to envision the textured, inconsistent complexity of the network. Challenges and opportunities uncovered during execution often cannot be passed on in real time to the appropriate planners. Unable to predict what the future will bring and lacking the ability to work with the unfolding reality, executives and companies find that what they desire has little resemblance to reality and that what gets done is at odds with what was desired.

How Ericsson Hit the Plan-and-Execute Wall (and Why the Midas Touch Did Not Help)

When Mr. Nilsson returned to Sweden from his diagnostic trip, he ran headlong into the Execution Trap. He sought and received Board approval to initiate a transformation of Ericsson. An objective assessment of the changes he sought would rate them as quintessentially solid, competent management strategies taught in business schools and in books read by practicing managers. But it did not work out that way.

The first trend of the new epoch—the decomposition of work over time and geography—springs the Execution Trap, because the different workgroups that are collaborating have to be linked coherently with flows of material, information, and money. If only three workgroups are linked, there will be only three flows of material, information, and money. However, as the number of networked workgroups grows, the number of flows grows even faster. When 10 groups are linked, there are 45 flows; when 20 groups collaborate, 190 flows must be managed. While I am certainly overstating the case (because in real life, every workgroup will not be linked to every other), *the undeniable fact is that as more groups of people work together, the numbers of flows of material, information, and money that must be coordinated rise rapidly.*

Mr. Nilsson accurately diagnosed the fact that Ericsson's vast, truly global operating network was under considerable strain. To give managers who had the most visibility into business issues commensurate authority, he decentralized decision-making. He gave geographic managers the authority to make key decisions that had hitherto been referred to senior executives and/or Sweden. To ensure coordinated action across the company as a whole, he asked these managers to provide more comprehensive reports to headquarters. These actions should have helped (and perhaps would have with time), but they created confusion at the start.[10]

Additionally, Mr. Nilsson recognized that Ericsson had to become much more lean; it had too many employees and very high expenses. So, he began eliminating personnel and assets and consolidating suppliers and slashing inventory. This step might have been necessary, but it probably also had a detrimental impact: In a complex network of workgroups, it can reduce, if not eliminate, any ability to effectively maneuver in the face of an unexpected challenge. Nevertheless, one should not single out Ericsson for criticism; many, perhaps most, large companies embark on such ill-named "Lean Sigma" programs, hijacking an approach developed to improve operations and using it to generate quick profits by "eliminating unproductive capital."

The second trend, that of extreme variety and/or customization, compounds the managerial challenges posed by the multiplicity of flows. For example, to create customized products, companies increasingly turn to using custom material. Among the North American companies I surveyed, 48% reported buying "more or much more" custom materials than they did before. Doing so has the unintended consequence of reducing substitutability; if something goes wrong in one shipment of a custom product, it is hard to create an identical replacement. Again, the ability of a network to execute a planned maneuver declines.

Mr. Nilsson saw no choice but to expand the variety of phones that Ericsson had to produce to compete effectively in a hypersegmented world. So he restructured Ericsson's approach to product development, going to the level of putting in place policies such as mandating "voice of the customer" studies in existing and future projects. Again, it is hard to find fault with an action that is extolled by every business school in the world. But as I will discuss in Chapter 6, "Ensure That Work Teaches," companies often struggle with—and even reject— process changes that seem incompatible with culture and structure. This struggle can become particularly painful in a networked world simply because of the multitude of workgroups and flows. And Ericsson certainly struggled to absorb this change.

Finally, the trend toward the blurring of industries further exacerbates the challenges of planning and executing in a networked world. In my study, 74% of the companies reported that they were seeking more or much more innovation *from outside their traditional supplier base*. For managers, the biggest implication of this statistic is that companies used to dealing with the norms and demands of one industry now *also* have to scramble to understand, adopt, and apply the norms and demands of others. In terms of the network model, not only do the numbers of workgroups and flows expand, but the actual information, monies, and material that have to flow also change. The resultant uncertainty and ambiguity impede planning and execution.

For Ericsson, this challenge was big enough to warrant explicit discussion in its 1999 annual report. In the telecommunications business, the norm had been to respond to well-defined requests for proposals from government agencies and regulated quasi-monopolies with bidding documents that "...occupied several meters of shelf space and took months for a team of skilled engineers to prepare." That, the annual report noted, "...was what the telecom world was like ten years ago. Just about what it was like 50 years ago." As this process got replaced by fast-moving competition among well-financed private and public companies, Ericsson had to sharply change its approach to business and restructure its workforce. It expected that the "...ten years ahead will bring even greater changes." The global organizational restructuring, which used geography rather than line of business to group people, was also supposed to help with this challenge by forcing fixed-line and mobile businesses to report to the same regional managers.

Mr. Nilsson also beefed up Ericsson's internal investments in technology and aggressively began acquiring technologies and small companies in order to deal with the convergence of telecommunications and the Internet. Ericsson entered into many software- and product-based partnerships with companies like Microsoft and Electrolux. The former was to develop and exploit "...total solutions for wireless Internet access...," and the latter was to "...research, develop and market products with access to the Internet to private homes."[11]

For a while, Mr. Nilsson's plan-and-execute strategy seemed to work. That year (1998) Ericsson's revenues rose 10%, and market capitalization rose 29%. It also sold 50% more phones than it did in 1997.

But under the surface, a number of facts caused heads to shake and tongues to wag. *Growth* in phone sales slowed (the year-end growth was 7%), and market share trended downward very gently. As a result, by the third quarter, Ericsson had to warn the markets of an impending loss of twelve thousand jobs and of a financial weakness that would continue into 1999. The T28 World Phone was meant to be a crucial launch for the company; it was being designed to serve as a platform that could be customized and introduced to meet the needs of different markets around the world. Despite the execution of the new plans, the project experienced a six-to-nine-month delay. Other product-development problems also emerged, and Ericsson did not effectively communicate these to the financial markets. Finally, perhaps because of, or in spite of, Ericsson's efforts to go Lean (I could not discern the truth here), in 1999 and 2000, just before and after the fire, Ericsson experienced serious component shortages.

After the glory years of the Ramqvist era, the financial markets found this performance unacceptable. In mid-1999, after a rocky eighteen-month tenure during which analysts found fault with almost all of Mr. Nilsson's decisions, Mr. Ramqvist fired him. Scathing criticism continued. The *Wall Street Journal* stated that he got the CEO's job only because his former boss, Kurt Hellström, had turned it down.[12] Noting that the organizational changes had caused many Ramqvist stalwarts to resign, the *Journal* suggested that Mr. Ramqvist had regarded the changes as a personal attack and had made several headline-grabbing statements that undercut Mr. Nilsson.

So was Mr. Nilsson simply a lousy manager? An objective reading of the evidence shows otherwise. Mr. Ramqvist added the CEO title again, and the Board appointed his longtime protégé, Mr. Hellström, president. They promised to restore Ericsson to health by year-end, and the business media started reporting stories of their many prior successes. *CNN Money* reported that Ericsson employees cheered their return.[13] *Forbes* lauded Mr. Hellström, saying, "Mr. Hellström is back, and Ericsson will be the better for it."[14] It reported that when Mr. Hellström gave an order, people followed it without question. Had Mr. Nilsson been on the wrong track, these men with the presumed Midas touch would certainly have changed course. They did not, and with the Board's explicit endorsement, they stuck with, and indeed accelerated, the implementation of Mr. Nilsson's plans. And for a while, until before the fire, these moves seemed to deliver the desired results. Strong planning and great execution seemed to characterize Ericsson once more, and the analysts were soothed.

In the aftermath of the fire, however, the analysts' tone again changed markedly. On July 20, 2000, when Ericsson reported on the financial impact of the fire, its share price dropped by 7% in Europe and 11% in the U.S. This happened despite the fact that the company as a whole earned pretax profits of over $2 billion—*39% higher than the market's expectations*.[15] Analysts tore apart its management. One news report called Ericsson "accident prone" and quoted one analyst as saying, "It proves Ericsson can't handle consumer products" and another as saying that the Consumer Products Division's numbers were "sheer and utter madness."[16] Others called Mr. Ramqvist's return as CEO a symptom of instability in the ranks of the senior-most executives.[17]

On October 19, Ericsson announced its third-quarter results: profits slightly exceeded market expectations and were 223% higher than the comparable nine months of 1999. Yet these could not cover the taint of the continuing and mounting losses in the mobile phone business.[18] Ericsson's share price plummeted 26% during intraday trading, but it recovered to be down only 16% for the day. By late January 2001, its share price stood 50% below its prefire level.

In January 2001, Mr. Ramqvist returned to being chairman, while Mr. Hellström became CEO. They held several senior executives accountable for Ericsson's failures to execute their plans.[19] Even so, they themselves couldn't live up to their image of being men with the Midas touch. Though Ericsson cut costs and shed 20% of its workforce, its mobile phone business hemorrhaged red ink. This limited its ability to finance purchases of telecommunications infrastructure products. By mid-March 2001, its shares plummeted a further 20% in a single day, pushing Nokia's shares down by 9% and taking the NASDAQ stock index below 2000.[20] Soon after, Ericsson announced another round of layoffs and factory closures and warned of still more reorganizations in April.

Swedish politicians began criticizing management, and rumors of employees and small shareholders asking for Mr. Ramqvist's and Mr. Hellström's firing surfaced.[21] In early April 2001, *Business Week* blamed Swedish laws for giving Ericsson's founders, the Wallenberg family, more power over management than was warranted by their minority shareholder status.[22] It blamed Mr. Ramqvist for returning, saying he had given Mr. Nilsson "little breathing room" and had been "largely invisible lately, even while [Mr.] Hellström takes the heat." It argued that "As the company's top leader, Mr. Ramqvist should be held responsible for Ericsson's inability to make tough decisions, such as failing to exit its doomed handset business, which cost the company $2.4 billion last year." It reported that key stakeholders wanted to "...replace [Mr.] Ramqvist, but it won't be easy..."

In May, Mr. Hellström responded by granting *Business Week* an interview about his views of Ericsson's problems:[23]

> When I took over, I realized that costs were way too high and expectations of growth far too optimistic. I started to realize that management didn't know what they were talking about. I put new guys in charge of that. I saw the product program was not that strong.

Unfortunately, the world changed in another way. Everybody was very optimistic, and we were very optimistic [about demand. Then, the market] started to shift to entry-level phones. That made our product not fit demand. We had to compete by lowering prices on high-end products. [New factories came online, so] capacity grew while demand dropped. So there was very, very heavy under-absorption which hit us. Then we had a fire that lost 7 million phones.

Mr. Hellström's plan-and-execute approach, which had served him well in the past, by his own admission, had failed in the new environment. *Business Week* did not seem to like Mr. Hellström's odds for turning Ericsson around.[24]

In late October, as mobile phone sales continued to fall and the company looked ready to report its first annual loss in fifty years, Michael Treschow, the CEO of consumer durables company Electrolux, replaced Mr. Ramqvist on the Board.[25] In 2002, excluding restructuring costs, Ericsson returned to profitability, but barely. Late in the year, Ericsson's shares bottomed out and began a slow recovery. Nevertheless, in January 2003, Mr. Hellström stepped down from the Board. The fourth CEO in five years, Carl-Henric Svanberg, took over. A year later, he declared victory, albeit on behalf of a much smaller company.

So should we conclude that Mr. Ramqvist and Mr. Hellstöm were also lousy managers and that Ericsson only now has a competent executive—Mr. Svanberg—in charge? Again, this indictment is baseless. These executives led a very successful company for years and had spectacular successes under their belts. I cannot imagine that they woke up one day and became unable to tie their own shoes! I tried, but I could not reach anyone senior at Ericsson to share their views, so I will offer on their behalf the only defense I can.

First, it is worth keeping in mind that after the fire, despite all the turmoil, Ericsson shipped 43.3 million phones, an increase of 38% in the number of units and 21% in sales. Though Nokia's growth rates of

64% and 67%, respectively, were far stronger, in any other environment, Ericsson's performance would have been called impressive. Even more remarkably, unable to find an alternative to Philips, within months, Ericsson modified one of its own Swedish factories to produce the affected chip. Second, in the spring of 2002, I spent eight hours over two days—pretty much one on one—with one of Ericsson's most senior executives. Our conversation ranged from the rapidity with which third-generation (3G) technologies would become commonplace to what Ericsson was doing to become adaptive. One executive does not make a company, but this gentleman was articulate and thoughtful and clearly understood the issues that Ericsson and the industry faced. He did not fit the caricature of the bumbling Ericsson executive crafted by some.

In reality, Ericsson had fallen headfirst into the Execution Trap. Mr. Nilsson and his successors took sensible steps but did not seem to realize that by itself, the plan-and-execute philosophy was no longer sufficient. The three megatrends associated with the epoch of distributed computer networks had dramatically increased the difficulty of planning-and-executing work. This was true regardless of the arena—manufacturing or sales or R&D or technology creation—in which work was performed. In each case, planning and executing had to take into account many, many more interconnected links. Each link brought with it not only great value, but also great, unexpected, unplanned challenges. Given their reduced visibility, executives and managers could not do what they needed to.

Small wonder, then, that planning has become an exercise in fantasy and execution a chase after the fantasy on a wing and a prayer. Based on a survey of large companies, Michael Mankins and Richard Steele wrote in the *Harvard Business Review*, "Companies typically realize only about 60% of their strategies' potential value because of defects and breakdowns in planning and execution."[26] They noted that if a sequence of annual plans of a typical large company were placed side by side, one would observe a series of hockey-stick projections. If actual performance were projected across these, one would see a smooth, relatively flat line, hugging the inflection points at the bottom of the sticks. Plainly stated, Mr. Mankins and Mr. Steele believe that most strategic plans are pipe dreams.

Yet, companies and managers have not stopped worshipping at the altar of plan and execute. Even Mr. Mankins' and Mr. Steele's recommended solution, like that of many other gurus, does not advocate fundamental change. Instead, it urges companies to make their strategic plans far more concrete and to adopt policies and monitoring systems to ensure that managers are very disciplined about executing these plans. In other words, to correct the failure of planning and execution to add value, companies should improve their planning and execution! I believe that the solution must lie elsewhere.

Ironically, under Mr. Nilsson, Ericsson's management team seemed to have understood the real challenge. The 1999 annual report also noted the following:

> Restructuring is a word that Ericsson and other companies in the industry will need to learn to live with. Tomorrow's winners will be the companies that are the best at change and best in reallocating competence and resources.
>
> ...distinct and proactive management and smart working methods will unquestionably be needed to provide the flexibility the market demands. But above all, an open mind will be required...the business culture must be one that encourages change and seeks opportunities in change.

Unfortunately, they did not pursue far enough the implications of their understanding. The Adaptive Business epoch had arrived. The world had changed—and will continue to do so. Ericsson was brittle and ready to break; the fire in March 2000 was merely a catalyst. In its one-hundred-year history, Ericsson had gone from strength to strength in each new market it entered, planning what it wanted to achieve, and executing against those plans. Nothing had prepared it to even consider the possibility that this approach had become obsolete.

Ericsson thus became one of the first high-profile victims of the most recent epochal change.

Why We Should Hold off on the Self-Congratulatory Backslapping

Most other companies, particularly large and global ones, are not off the hook. Figure 2-1 summarizes a key finding of the study I conducted on North American companies: Many (albeit not the majority) faced "frequent" and/or "severe" problems when confronted with a range of specific day-to-day operating challenges.

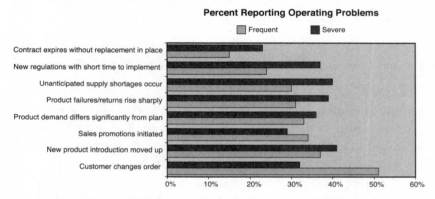

Figure 2-1   The prevalence of severe and/or frequent problems in 350 U.S. manufacturing companies.

A close review of this data should—must!—startle everyone. Customers change their minds—regularly. Sales promotions happen—regularly. New product introductions get moved up in response to changes in the competitive landscape—regularly. Unanticipated supply shortages occur—regularly. Product demand differs significantly from plan—regularly. Though none are of the magnitude of a fire disabling a key supplier, all these *predictable* events continue to strain the abilities of our leading companies. Many well trained, well disciplined, well managed, well equipped standing armies are finding their might tested by enemies that are changeable in form and battlefields that are not of their choosing. So too are companies that rely solely on plan-and-execute methodologies troubled by customers who change their minds and competitive actions that force the moving up of new-product introductions—and fires that shut down suppliers' operations.

In reality, then, many major companies today are not unlike Ericsson was before the fire. Their plan-and-execute approach makes them brittle. Faced with a challenge as large as the one Ericsson did, they too could falter. The truth of the matter is that if they look in the mirror, senior executives of many more companies should say silent prayers to whichever management or spiritual deity they believe in and offer thanks that their companies have not found themselves in Ericsson's situation (yet).

So, You Are Not the CEO...

Before you can do anything, you need to know where your business unit stands vis-à-vis the issues I have raised here. Unless your business unit is completely atypical, chances are the challenges and opportunities you see around you will be replicated to a greater or lesser extent throughout your company. So, at the very least, changes that you think you need may make your own business unit an Adaptive Business. If all goes well, they may play a part in the holographic implementation I describe in Chapter 9, "Introduce Change Holographically."

Specifically:

1. Using the final four columns of Table 2-1 for guidance, determine which epoch your business unit operates in, and evaluate your managerial policies.

2. Compared to two years ago, where does your business stand with respect to the impact of the three trends?

3. Evaluate the effectiveness of your planning process and your performance against your plans. What, if anything, would you change if you could?

4. If you were asked to defend specific things you did (for example, pursuing a particular deal), not on the basis of their impact on your performance metrics, but on the basis of their adherence to your strategy, how would you rate your performance?

5. Do you think you are in the grips of the Execution Trap? How would you make a case for or against this concept?

6. Could you put together a business case for change to present to your boss or peers?

Endnotes

[1] Jai was the chairman of my doctoral thesis committee. He passed away prematurely of a heart attack in February 1998 while pursuing his lifelong passion of mountain climbing.

[2] The original working paper that Jai had hoped to turn into a book is not readily accessible. A close alternative is the book of the same name, *From Filing and Fitting to Flexible Manufacturing*, by Ramchandran Jaikumar, Now Publishers, May 2005, ISBN 1-933019-06-9. It is available from http://www.nowpublishers.com. Professor Roger Bohn, a friend and colleague of Jai's, edited this version for posthumous publication.

[3] "Quality on the Line," by David Garvin, *Harvard Business Review*, September–October, 1983.

[4] "Postindustrial Manufacturing," by Ramchandran Jaikumar, *Harvard Business Review*, November 1, 1986.

[5] "Outsourcing Innovation," by Pete Engardio and Bruce Einhorn, *Business Week*, March 21, 2005.

[6] Ultimately, the system was not made because unrelated business reasons kept the Fortune 500 company that was our partner from taking this new product to market.

[7] As recently as 1993, a group of INSEAD business school professors (including me) refereed an argument between the managers of Philips' erstwhile white-goods division and its American acquirer, Whirlpool. The latter argued that twelve days of raw material in the French plants constituted an unacceptable use of capital. Supplies for American factories came from farther away, yet inventory levels were lower. The Europeans argued that the U.S. did not have customs inspection at state boundaries; the French-Italian border was particularly notorious for delays. Some "just in case" inventory was essential to ensure that the factories did not grind to a halt.

[8]The sample sizes for each of these responses varied from just over 150 to over 400, assuring the statistical reliability of the findings.

[9]Ericsson 1999 Annual Report, p. 5.

[10]"Swedish Massage," by Richard Heller, Forbes.com, September 20, 1999.

[11]Ericsson 1999 Annual Report, p. 14.

[12]"Ericsson's Nilsson learns it's tough to succeed a leader who stays on," the *Wall Street Journal*, July 13, 1999.

[13]"Stock gains through Swedish phone firm posts unexpectedly high profit slump," *CNN Money*, July 23, 1999.

[14]Ibid, Forbes.com.

[15]"Ericsson's Mobile Worries," BBC, July 21, 2000, 21:35 GMT, 22:35 UK, http://news.bbc.co.uk/2/hi/business/845619.stm.

[16]European Newswatch, July 21, 2000.

[17]For example, see European Newswatch, July 21, 2000, which noted, "Equally clear is that last July's internal management shake-up, which saw the then company president Mr. Ramqvist return to executive duties, has not been enough to set the group on an even keel, at least in the consumer area."

[18]"Ericsson's Mobile Woes," BBC, October 20, 2000, 16:51 GMT, 17:51 UK, news.bbc.co.uk/2/hi/business/981075.stm.

[19]"Big IT companies continue to cut personnel," Helsingin Sanomat International Edition, *Business & Finance*, February 19, 2001.

[20]"Ericsson profit warning causes Nokia share to crash," Helsingin Sanomat International Edition, *Business & Finance*, March 13, 2001.

[21]"Ericsson and Nokia announce personnel layoffs," Helsingin Sanomat International Edition, *Business & Finance*, March 28, 2001.

[22]"Why Ericsson Is Bleeding," *Business Week*, April 2, 2001.

[23]"Interview with CEO Kurt Hellström," *Business Week*, May 7, 2001 (Online Extra).

[24]"Can CEO Hellstrom reverse its fading fortunes?" *Business Week*, May 7, 2001.

[25]"Earnings shock for Ericsson," BBC, October 26, 2001, 07:14 GMT, 08:14 UK, http://news.bbc.co.uk/2/hi/business/1620709.stm.

[26]"Turning Great Strategy into Great Performance," by Michael Mankins and Richard Steele, *Harvard Business Review*, July–August 2005.

3

Visions from the Present

The English language—like many others, I suppose—has sayings that simultaneously sound trite, paternalistic, and pompous to many ears. Once in a while, one of these sayings actually comes true and pokes its finger in our eye. One such saying is, "What does not kill you may make you stronger." It accurately captures how and why Nokia became adaptive.

During the mid-1990s, Nokia was going through unprecedented change. Under CEO Jorma Ollila, it was busy reinventing itself as a global player in telecommunications by selling off businesses and investments in all other areas, including, for example, electrical power, tires, and chemicals. In parallel, it was growing its telecommunications infrastructure and mobile phones businesses at rates in excess of 50% annually. By year-end 1995, the telephony business accounted for 71% of its $8.4 billion in revenues and was expected to rise to 100%.

Nokia was also coping with the three trends of the emerging Adaptive Business epoch. By year-end 1995, it had become the world's second-largest mobile phone maker. It sold phones in 120 countries, supplying one in five phones sold worldwide. It focused single-mindedly on distinguishing among the needs of different types of customers; its annual reports for the rest of the decade prominently featured the term "segmentation." It entered new markets, particularly in Asia, though it had historically not had huge sales there. It took newly available digital mobile phone technology to the sophisticated Japanese market and helped establish digital phones in China. It also

kept a foot firmly planted on the analog side of the product and technology fence so that it could enter nascent markets like India. Believing that the emerging 2G technology would cause technologically
sophisticated customers to defer purchases, it created a "future-proof"
line of phones to help them bridge the generational divide.

This geographic, product line, and technological expansion
needed support from a complex supply-and-demand network. Nokia
created sales offices and adapted to the myriad of distribution channels in place across the world. A new distribution center came online
in Singapore. As its plants in Finland, Germany, the United States,
Hong Kong, and South Korea began to feel capacity constraints,
Nokia opened new plants in Finland and the U.S. and signed agreements to build two more plants in China. By year-end 1995, it manufactured phones on four continents. It had also established strategic
alliances for technology and product development with major electronics manufacturers in the U.S., Asia, and Europe and opened a new
R&D center in Japan. Hiring by manufacturing, sales, marketing, and
R&D functions caused Nokia's head count to grow 20%.

Through all this change, Nokia followed an old-fashioned plan-
and-execute model that did not even incorporate Lean Enterprise
principles. Pertti Korhonen described its challenges:

> It was very traditional. Sales, distribution, manufacturing,
> procurement, they were all operating in functional silos. Dis-
> tribution was sending internal purchase orders to manufactur-
> ing...There was not one plan, but many plans. Sales had a plan.
> Distribution had a plan. Manufacturing had a plan...And there
> we were, executing to these plans.

Nokia's management recognized these weaknesses but had not
been able to make needed changes, in part because of political conflicts that affect all large organizations. Mr. Korhonen:

> The company had tried to reengineer the supply chain two,
> three times, but it did not work. The line organizations, func-
> tional organizations had power. The people who tried to bring

an end-to-end view were not strong enough. Or there wasn't a crisis big enough to change the silos. In 1995, the management...came to the conclusion that something had to be done.

This realization occurred when the three trends ultimately conspired to cause Nokia to stumble seriously. Mr. Korhonen:

> ...the company's product portfolio was getting old...and...there was a dip in our competitiveness...These...created a situation of increasingly large inventories of wrong components and shortage of the right components. At the same time, the product portfolio was being changed, and we did not have the components we needed for the new products.

In contrast to the aftermath of the fire five years later, this stumbling did make it into the 1995 Annual Report. In his letter to shareholders, Mr. Ollila wrote, "Some growth pains were felt..." The Review by the Board of Directors expanded on the issue, albeit elliptically:

> Despite strong sales growth, Nokia Mobile Phones' profitability was adversely affected by a number of factors...The principal factor...was the difficulty of meeting the challenges created by the business group's rapid growth.... Nokia Mobile Phones introduced substantial new production and distribution capacity, while hiring a significant number of new employees in order to meet expected demand. Profitability was also affected by factors associated with the rapid growth of Nokia and the industry in general, including interruptions in the supply of certain components, as well as logistical issues. Consequently, the business group experienced certain difficulties in bringing this production capacity and logistics associated therewith up to optimal levels.

In retrospect, what happened was eerily similar to Ericsson's experiences in 2000. Nokia could not produce enough phones and lost millions of dollars of potential sales. As such, though divisional sales grew 44%, overheads associated with planned growth drove down the divisional operating margin from 16% to 11%.

Mr. Ollila then took a set of steps that had a major impact on Nokia's future. Working with Matti Alahuhta, president of the mobile phone division, he appointed Mr. Korhonen, a vice president in Nokia's European manufacturing function who had worked in R&D for the bulk of his career, the divisional head of logistics. He charged Mr. Korhonen with finding a solution that would preclude the recurrence of such a failure. In his letter to the shareholders, he vowed:

> Given the ever-changing nature of the telecommunications industry, our ambition to instill the spirit of continuous learning in all new employees will be a key factor in our future success.

And so began Nokia's transformational journey. Mr. Ollila and Mr. Alahuhta made the gutsy decision to appoint an atypical manager to handle Nokia's challenge. For his part, not having been exposed to the received wisdom in this area, Mr. Korhonen looked beyond the prevailing plan-and-execute philosophy. Supported by Mr. Ollila and Mr. Alahuhta, he made several key decisions that enabled Nokia to acquire its adaptive capabilities.

The Power of Networks

Not too long ago, businesses functioned as hierarchical entities internally and as linear supplier-customer chains externally. In Chapter 2, "Shadows of the Past," I began arguing that the three mega trends associated with the present epoch have substantially changed the playing field, producing networks of companies that must work with each other. Indeed, since the late 1990s, I have been urging executives to think of *the network of companies* that surrounds them, *for their emergence is the defining organizational characteristic of our times.*

These networks did not emerge suddenly but are part of a well established pattern. This is apparent from Table 3-1, a modified version of Table 2-1, which summarized Ramchandran Jaikumar's epochal analysis. (Consistent with Chapter 2, I included CIM in the fifth epoch and called the sixth Adaptive Business.) The fourth column gives the total number of people in a typical production setting in each epoch. This number rose for the first three epochs (130 years) to three hundred people, stabilized at three hundred for the fourth, and has been dropping for about fifty years now. The fifth column shows that during the last seventy-five years or so, increasingly diverse groups of people have been working collaboratively. During the Dynamic Control epoch, people first worked in problem-solving teams within their own functional areas and then later across adjacent areas. During the Numeric Control epoch, as microprocessors entered the workplace, even broader groups of people—spanning manufacturing, engineering, and product development—worked together.

In the Adaptive Business epoch, we are seeing rapid extensions of these trends. Marketers, salespeople, finance professionals, and logistics experts are working with manufacturers or engineers to create products (and services). We call the groups they work within names that were unknown not too long ago: "centers of excellence," "communities of practice," "lateral links," and "process organizations." Many of these exist within a company's boundaries, but because of the increasing decomposition of work and the blurring of industries, they cross organizational lines very frequently.

Why should senior general managers care about this, instead of leaving its management to functional experts and mid-level managers? Simply because in every prior epoch, changes in business structure created new winners and losers among companies. Thus, it is reasonable to expect that the change in structure engendered by this epoch will affect companies similarly.

TABLE 3-1   Jai's Epochs of Manufacturing, with the Last Two Epochs Changed

	Epochs		Managerial Changes			
Era	Name	Technological Drivers	How Many People / % Staff	Changes in Organization Structure	How Work Is Transformed	Ethos: What Is Valued
Before 1800	Make, not Manufacture				Master inspects	Artisan skills
1789– 1800	English System	Flat plane, micrometer, drawings	40 / 0%	Guilds break up	Worker inspects	Accuracy in mechanical craft
1798– 1855	American System	Specialized machines, gauges	150 / 13%	Quality control, use of outside contractors	Foremen supervise work tightly	Precision in repetitive work
1890– 1920	Scientific Management	Stopwatch, job studies, empirical data	300 / 20%	Jobs specialized by function	Foremen supervise work lightly and problems closely	Decompose and deskill work
1930s– 1960	Dynamic Control	SPC charts, semiautomated machines	300 / 33%	Problem-solving teams formed	Workers assess problems, supervisors lightly review	Diagnose problems
1940s– 1990s	Numeric Control/ Computer-Integrated Manufacturing	Microprocessors and automatic tool changing, CAD, CAM, FMS	100 / 50%	Multiple functions integrated	Limited or no supervision	Experiment to improve
1990s–?	Adaptive Business	Distributed computer networks	30 / 67%	Dispersed, networked workgroups	Limited or no supervision across workgroups	Learn, generalize, and share

The perfect example of this kingmaking power of networks is Apple, Inc., which, in less than a decade, went from being a highly innovative also-ran to a respected and hugely profitable company. Not long ago, Apple existed in a linear world. It bought chips from IBM and drives and components from a handful of others. It nagged

Microsoft to continue to support Office and Internet Explorer for the Mac and begged other companies not to give up on the Mac platform. It sold the Macintosh largely online and through a rapidly shrinking base of retailers.

Today, Apple is creating brilliant, iconic, highly profitable products and services by placing itself in the midst of a network of companies that span six (converging) industries: computers, consumer electronics, telecommunications, music, television, and film. It is no longer dependent on the largess of Microsoft. It works with companies including Intel (for chips), AT&T (for telephony), most music companies, several TV networks (like ABC), several movie producers, home entertainment systems makers (like Bose), and makers of numerous auxiliary systems (like Shure). It partnered with a partial rival (Hewlett-Packard) to take an HP-branded iPod to market. It expanded its distribution system, not just by opening a network of high-end retail stores, but also by working with big-box retailers like Costco. In short, Apple created a new network of retailers, distributors, technology creators, and suppliers to complement and reenergize the one it had.

Apple's experience ratifies the advice I have been giving managers for almost ten years. To be successful, they must effectively manage workgroups that fulfill four distinct but interlocking roles:

- **Build markets:** These workgroups are essential for selling products. Great market builders use their own brand names or market power to provide priority access to target customers.
- **Create technologies:** These workgroups create key, distinctive intellectual property. Great technology creators understand the evolving worlds of their customers and—in a world consumed by battles over ownership—respect their *partners'* intellectual property rights.
- **Assure supply:** These workgroups obtain or manufacture critical components and systems. Strong supply assurors have deep process capabilities and create high-quality goods at reasonable prices.

- **Develop complementary resources:** These workgroups provide ancillary products and services that, although inessential, engender great success or, in their absence, instigate failure. Great complementary resource developers possess deep insights into customer behavior; invaluable ones also raise customers' *barriers to exit* with their contributions.[1]

A workgroup may be internal, but it is increasingly a distinct external company. Many different workgroups typically perform each role, but a single workgroup may perform more than one role. In particular, overlaps in market and supply roles, market and technology roles, and technology and complementary resource roles are common. For example, Matsushita is both supply assuror and technology creator for Nokia. Collectively, these internal and external workgroups make up a company's network.

Not every company that provides such capabilities is important. Indeed, defining who is (and why) is a critically important managerial task. The important ones are worthy of being called "partners"; most of the ideas in this book apply to them. In Apple's network, for example, AT&T proved to be a key player, collaborating as a market builder and complementary resource developer in the effort to take the iPhone to market. At Nokia, sixty companies account for 90% of purchases, and a mere ten companies account for 60%. Of these sixty, Nokia has extremely close relationships with five companies and close relationships with twelve to fifteen more. In other words, over two-thirds of its suppliers are members of Nokia's network, but only a handful are supply-assuring and technology-creating partners.

The New Capabilities of an Adaptive Business

Because of the need to fill these different roles in environments separated by time and space, members of a network may differ radically in size, goals, values, cultures, organizational structures, processes, risk tolerance, and a host of other factors.[2] Such mis-matches mean that very often amorphous, uneven groups that march to the beats of different drums must work together. Their collaboration must deal in real time with the implications of such differences: what a given workgroup notices in its environment, what it considers important, whether and how it reacts to these, and what it does. In the hours and days after the fire, for example, Nokia, Ericsson, and Philips clearly displayed divergent attitudes toward risk. The most comprehensive contractual agreements in the world cannot address some of these mismatches. This is particularly true when the mismatches arise from cultural differences or differences in the preparedness and ability to learn about ambiguous or highly uncertain situations.

As such, managers and executives operating in this environment lack considerable—and sometimes complete—visibility into, and control over, critical events that may affect specific partners and/or the overall network. Nor can they seal off their workgroups from problems or opportunities that arise in another workgroup within their network, because information, monies, and products must flow incessantly from one to another.

In effect, each workgroup's fortunes get inextricably intertwined with those of others. This implies that, *by and large, members of networks win or lose together; rarely can a company succeed while its network is failing.* In other words, we are now in a world of *network-based competition*.

Apple's story presents the positive face of what this means. In contrast, in 2001–2002, Bristol-Meyers Squibb provided a textbook example of network mismanagement.[3] In mid-2001, it abruptly (and, in retrospect, wrongly) terminated an agreement with Novartis to jointly promote a potentially blockbuster drug when regulators raised some concerns. In September, it agreed to pay $2 billion to cement a partnership with ImClone, a small biotech company. It clearly did so without sufficient due diligence, for by December, regulators turned down ImClone's application for the drug BMS hoped to take to market, and

BMS got dragged into a highly visible insider trading scandal. By April 2002, BMS struggled with a sharp decline in purchases by its wholesalers; past stuffing of the distribution channels (which resulted in an accounting probe) had left the wholesalers with greater inventories than they needed.

If the plan-and-execute approach of prior epochs is inadequate for network-based competition, what *is* needed? Individual workgroups—and the network as a whole—must develop three *additional* capabilities that complement plan and execute:

- **The ability to *sense*, or detect, unexpected changes.** Not everything will go as planned. Capabilities must be built to obtain insights into the possible pleasant and unpleasant surprises from other workgroups and the general business environment. Doing so is very difficult for two reasons: *ex ante*, it may not be apparent what insights might be needed, and as the autonomy of the other workgroups rise, sensing will require their active cooperation.

- **The ability to *respond to*, or act on, the unexpected changes.** To act on what it senses, the workgroup/network must tackle the difficult task of creating the capability to act if and when an unknown event happens. Doing so requires creativity, determination, and, quite possibly, the agreement of—and active cooperation from—other groups in the network.

- **The ability to *learn from* experience, intelligently generalize, and share the lessons.** A workgroup must be able to learn from prior occurrences of similar events. Moreover, a challenge or opportunity that is novel for one workgroup may well be routine for another. As such, the entire network will function effectively if its workgroups create the means to capture and quickly transfer lessons learned to each other. This capability also presupposes active cooperation among partners.

Figure 3-1 captures the essence of an Adaptive Business. It shows these five capabilities—Plan, Execute, Sense, Respond, and Learn—tightly wound around each other, almost like two pairs of ribbons (Plan and Execute, and Sense and Respond) enveloping a ball (Learn). Just as a company cannot be adaptive without being able to sense, respond, and learn, it also cannot be adaptive without being able to plan and execute.

The five capabilities, working in concert, enable a company to consistently, effectively, and efficiently deal with small and large changes in its environment. When I first presented a very similar icon to Mr. Korhonen, he observed that it "...describe(d) exactly what Nokia is trying to do."

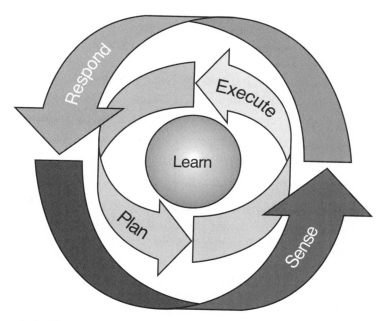

Figure 3-1   The Adaptive Business paradigm: Sense and Respond complements Plan and Execute, while Learn unifies the system.

Where Ericsson and Nokia Stood

Could these additional capabilities have helped Ericsson? No one can answer this question unequivocally, but we can speculate based on fragmentary evidence:

- Did Ericsson believe it was a part of a network? The supporting evidence is weak. After the fire, it could not draw on strong relations with others. Certainly the lesson it took away was that it should never be dependent on any one supplier again.

- Did Ericsson develop sense-and-respond capabilities? Under Sven-Christer Nilsson, by decentralizing decision-making and backing away from centralized planning and execution, it created workgroups with local autonomy. However, I could not tell if it went any further.

- Did Ericsson create capabilities to learn and transfer lessons across workgroups? Though Mr. Nilsson's merging of business lines should have facilitated this, after the fire, Ericsson did not seem to use any lessons learned to protect its infrastructure business. Either it ran out of time, or Mr. Nilsson's dismissal kept this change from doing the job it was supposed to.

In contrast, Nokia built these capabilities and therefore dealt with the fire in what Mr. Korhonen called a "business as usual" fashion. When I asked about the benefits of doing so, I posed the question hesitantly. I prefaced it with qualifiers about the impact of the economy, products, competitors, and governments on a business. His response was unhesitating and forthright:

> This year we will probably...ship more than 300 million phones. If you think about the effort needed to scale up a business to do this, if you look at how we are scaling up to reach these volumes, it is all about the network. *How the whole network works together is Nokia's greatest competitive advantage.*

Other Nokia executives made similar assertions. Hewlett-Packard executives also praised their partners' positive impact either directly or indirectly. However, I freely admit that it is hard, perhaps impossible, to assemble incontrovertible proof. There is no way to assess how a company (say, Nokia) would have performed if its network did not exist. Additionally, objective data may not be available at the required level of granularity to assess whether a company (say, HP) has implemented effective network management across some, but not all, business areas.

Nevertheless, financial data seems to indicate that Nokia's network allowed it to do much more with relatively fewer people and resources. In 2006 Nokia's revenues (over €41 billion) were 560% higher than its 1995 base telecommunications revenues (about €6 billion), while the operating profits were 550% higher. Outside the financial services industry, not many large companies have achieved this rate of *sustained, organic* growth. Simultaneously, Nokia's network held down—to only 100%—the growth in the number of people it employed. As such, revenues per employee rose by 230%, while operating profits per employee rose by 220%. The meltdown in the telecommunications industry *after* 2000 did dilute somewhat the network's impact. Compared to 2000, the 2006 revenues per employee were 19% higher, and operating profits per employee were 16% lower, but earnings per share per employee were 10% higher. Unadjusted for employees, the performance was stronger. Nokia's very strong financial performance during the first half of 2007 greatly strengthens this argument.

The Imperfect Judgments of Not-Quite-Perfect Markets

At this point, some executives may accept the *desirability* of the adaptive transformation but question the *urgency*. Others may accept both the desirability and the urgency, but may believe that the necessary changes can and should be tackled by functional and operating managers as a part of their everyday work.

I believe a different perspective is warranted. The examples and survey data in this book will show that many companies and industries are struggling in the new epoch, just as others struggled at the start of prior epochs. The changes they must initiate are so profound—and must be so widespread—that they must embark on a corporate transformation. Such a transformation is best guided, if not actively managed, from the top.

Years ago, I used to tell my MBA students, "Top managers don't have enough hours in a day to do everything you want them to do. If *everything* needs top management attention, *nothing* will get top management attention." My position here contradicts this view for good reason. Whether or not a company transforms itself quickly has an enormous impact on its financial performance. In the early years of the twenty-first century, financial markets are holding top managers accountable for perceived failures more than at any time in the past. If the transformation does not find room on top managers' agendas, their legacies could well be at risk. This issue, explored next, is the final element of the argument for change.

When Share Prices Fall...

A person who had invested SKR 1,000 in Ericsson shares just before the end of the third quarter of 1995 could have liquidated this investment for about SKR 10,000 in the days before the fire at Philips (see Figure 3-2). If he or she had not done so, by the second quarter of 2002, that investment would have been worth only about SKR 400. In fact, Ericsson's stock dropped 43% in the period starting just before the crisis and ending after it. Six months later, it still stood 56% below the pre-crisis level. (By late 2004, the original investment would have recovered somewhat and would have been worth about SKR 2,000.)

Kevin Hendricks and Vinod Singhal conducted a fascinating study that showed that such a pummeling is common. They studied how adverse events that fall within the purview of a general manager's responsibilities—production problems, parts shortages, order changes by customers, and problems in design and engineering—affected companies' share prices. Their initial study covered 519 North American companies from 1989 to 2000 (as the latest epoch emerged). It compared the change in share prices on the day a problem was announced to the price the day before.[4] On average:

- Such announcements brought a 10.3% price drop, and the shares did not recover for a quarter.
- Companies could not escape punishment by blaming others. If anything, the market responded most negatively when customers alone (14.3% drop) or a combination of customers and suppliers (10.9% drop) created the problem.

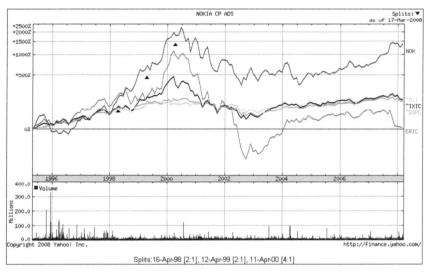

Figure 3-2 Share prices of Nokia and Ericsson, compared with the NASDAQ index, the Dow Jones Industrial Average, and the S&P index.

Clearly, the market punishes failure harshly—particularly failure across what I have called a company's network.

Having established this, Mr. Hendricks and Mr. Singhal broadened their focus to include two other common conditions.[5] The first is that sometimes, unlike the Philips fire, problems are not totally unexpected, but result from long-standing weaknesses. The markets can become aware of such deficiencies in advance of any crisis because of events like rising customer complaints or the buildup of inventories. The second condition addresses the idea that markets are not always as efficient as our standard theories assume. Unforeseen implications of a problem may become apparent only in the days and weeks after its announcement. Moreover, the markets may need extended periods of time to absorb the information they have been given.

Mr. Hendricks and Mr. Singhal conducted a slightly larger study (827 companies) of public American companies. Again, they focused on the period of emergence of the present epoch, 1989 to 2000. This time, they uncovered the true extent of the punishment that the markets imposed. A year after the announcement, share prices of affected companies generally stood between 35% and 41% below the levels reached a year before the announcement. Moreover, the shares showed no inclination to rise up to two years after the announcement!

Seen in the context of these analyses, the pattern of behavior in Ericsson's share prices seems perfectly reasonable. Ericsson's stock price actually continued to drop—and rather precipitously—even after it had supposedly isolated the mobile phone business, first by outsourcing some manufacturing (to Flextronics and others) and later by forming the joint venture with Sony. It seems as if the markets rightfully surmised that the problems highlighted by the fire also extended to Ericsson's infrastructure business, and fixing them would take time.

...So Do Reputations

By the end of 2002, the reputations of three Ericsson CEOs—Mr. Nilsson, Lars Ramqvist, and Kurt Hellström—and a few other senior managers had been damaged. Did these men deserve their tarring and feathering? Was it inappropriate for the markets to expect them to pull wizard's wands out of their pockets and wave them to heal Ericsson overnight? Conversely, if markets didn't hold top executives accountable for their companies' fortunes, how would they effectively represent shareholders?

Again, there is nothing unusual about the price these individuals paid. The consulting company Booz Allen Hamilton conducts an annual survey of CEO succession across the 2,500 largest global companies. The survey measures CEO performance using the yardstick of total shareholder returns (TSR), which combines share price changes and dividends.

The 2002 survey, titled "Deliver or Depart," noted that *two in five* of the departing CEOs left for performance-related reasons, compared to 20% in 2001.[6] Moreover, Boards judged their performance more strictly than in the prior couple of years. The TSR of dismissed CEOs lagged the TSR of CEOs who retired with honor by *only 6%*; the gap had been 12% in 2001 and 14% in 2000. This harsh treatment spanned the globe, as European and Asian Boards acted like their North American counterparts. The study asserted:

> The conclusion is inescapable: Forced CEO succession has become the "new normal." Boards of directors are now exercising their powers on behalf of shareholders with almost unprecedented vigor.

The 2004 Booz Allen Hamilton survey, titled "The World's Most Prominent Temp Workers," noted that overall, CEO transitions had risen sharply worldwide, and nearly *one in three* had been forcibly removed from office.[7] Moreover, despite the media focus on ethics scandals and criminal charges for senior executives,

> Underperformance—not ethics, not illegality, not power struggles—is the primary reason CEOs got fired. Forced turnovers are strongly correlated with poor shareholder performance.

The Boards were slightly more charitable than they had been in 2002; the TSR of dismissed CEOs lagged those of honorable retirees by 8%. However, European and Asian companies dismissed CEOs more frequently than did North American Boards. The study called the situation in Europe a crisis, for the average fired European CEO had served only two-and-a-half years, far too short a time to get any-thing substantial done.

One in seven CEOs left their jobs in 2005, 70% higher than in 1995. In North America, 35% left for performance reasons, a record; in Europe and Asia, such departures reached their second-highest lev-els.[8] Compared to 1995, "(t)he firing of underperformers quadru-pled." The 2007 study reported a stabilization in both the overall departure rates and those for poor performance, albeit at the much higher "new normal" rates reached during this decade.[9]

The Leadership Challenge

Reviewed objectively, the data in Figure 2-1 (on frequent and se-vere problems) show that despite widespread use of managerial tools like Lean Sigma and information technologies, large numbers of com-panies are struggling to deal with run-of-the-mill, everyday problems. Their predicament suggests that either they have not realized that they must change, or they have not figured out *how* to change. Sooner or later, several of these companies are likely to stumble, perhaps in market-moving ways. When this happens, the research done by Mr. Hendricks and Mr. Singhal and the surveys done by Booz Allen Hamilton show that the consequences for them and their top leaders are likely to be dire.

Therefore, companies must urgently endeavor to transform them-selves. The effort will be difficult and will take considerable time. It must happen even as financial markets continue to display their cus-tomary focus on the numbers. As such, executives who react proac-tively (as Mr. Ollila, Mr. Alahuhta, and Mr. Korhonen did at Nokia) may get no credit and may even be blamed for wasting resources (un-less, like Nokia, their companies pull off seeming miracles). Execu-tives who fail to react proactively (like Mr. Ramqvist) may see their reputations tarnished when their companies falter. And finally, execu-tives who see a looming crisis and try to rapidly make changes (like

Mr. Nilsson and Mr. Hellström) may be pilloried when they run out of time. The markets will turn a deaf ear to their explanations that orchestrating transformation during an epochal change takes time and demands patience.

Good management is often a thankless task. During epochal shifts, this fact becomes even more true. The Jai that I knew would have chuckled.

So, You Are Not the CEO...

You must make a critical *mind-set* change: stop thinking about chains, and start thinking about networks. This will be hard, because everything around you will conspire to drag you back: Work flowing from one person to another and the established business jargon—such as supply *chain* management—assumes linearity. But change you must, for only then can you change anyone or anything else.

Here are a few tangible things to do:

1. Map out your business unit's network of workgroups, internal and external. *Nothing* of importance ever gets done in a large company simply through formal lines of authority; informal power bases, alliances, and the like play critical roles. Include these in the map:

   - How diverse are the workgroups?

   - What could align them? What could lead to conflicting perspectives on key issues?

   - Which workgroups are good at planning? Execution?

2. Superimpose on your map two issues from the "So You Are Not the CEO..." sidebar in Chapter 2:

   - What would you need/like to sense?

   - What response capabilities would you like to develop?

   - What could get in the way of developing these capabilities?

3. How well do the workgroups share knowledge and learn? What gets in the way?

Pick two challenges that require sense-respond-learn capabilities. Consider how you would convince your peers and/or your boss to focus on these. Don't look for perfection; look to make things better. Limit your ideas to what is (collectively) doable instead of pursuing what you would like.

Endnotes

[1] Two examples illustrate the criticality of this role. Patent holders for one of the world's most ubiquitous kitchen appliances—the microwave oven—made no money because microwave-safe cookware and frozen foods formulated for microwave cooking emerged only as the patents neared expiration. In contrast, while the cost of an alternative MP3 player may not stop a consumer from abandoning Apple's iPod, that person's investment in iPod accessories might.

[2] For example, the network that I was helping build (see Chapter 2) had members of dramatically different sizes and cultures. My employer had fewer than 100 people but amazing intellectual property, well protected by patents. Our market-building partner was an American white-goods manufacturer with sales in the billions. Our technology-creating (and expected supply-assuring) partner was even larger and had little at stake in our success. However, our immediate work was with its hard-charging Indian subsidiary, which was not much larger than we were. Yet another supply-assuring partner was a Chinese manufacturer whose focus for the most part was on growing its well-known white-goods business within China. And we were trying to establish a complementary resource partnership with a food manufacturer that was one of the largest companies in the world.

[3] "CEO Full Count: Bristol-Myers Squibb's Peter R. Dolan," by Matthew Harper, *Forbes*, October 22, 2002.

[4] "The Effect of Supply Chain Glitches on Shareholder Value," by Kevin Hendricks and Vinod Singhal, *Journal of Operations Management*, Volume 21, Number 5, December 2003.

[5] "An Empirical Analysis of the Effects of Supply Chain Disruptions on the Long Term Stock Price Performance and Equity Risk of the Firm," by Kevin Hendricks and Vinod Singhal, *Production and Operations Management*, Volume 14, Number 1, 2005.

[6] "CEO Succession 2002: Deliver or Depart," by Chuck Lucier, Rob Schuyt, and Eric Spiegel, *Strategy + Business*, Issue 31, Booz Allen Hamilton.

[7]"CEO Succession 2004: The World's Most Prominent Temp Workers," by Chuck Lucier, Rob Schuyt, and Edward Tse, *Strategy + Business*, Issue 39, Booz Allen Hamilton.

[8]"CEO Succession 2005: The Crest of the Wave," by Chuck Lucier, Paul Kocourek, and Rolf Habbel, *Strategy + Business*, Issue 43, Booz Allen Hamilton.

[9]"CEO Succession 2007: The Era of the Inclusive Leader," by Chuck Lucier, Steven Wheeler, and Rolf Habbel, *Strategy + Business*, Issue 47, Booz Allen Hamilton.

Part II
Design Principles for Adaptive Capabilities

"As long as there have been humans, we have searched for our place in the cosmos. Where are we? Who are we? We find that we live on an insignificant planet of a humdrum star lost in a galaxy tucked away in some forgotten corner of a universe in which there are far more galaxies than people. We make our world significant by the courage of our questions and by the depth of our answers."

—Carl Sagan, *Cosmos*

4

Transform Everyday Work

American retailers call the day after Thanksgiving "Black Friday." The term harks back to times when most retailers moved on this day from red ink (losses) to black ink (profits) for the year. In our more sophisticated times, sales in the post-Thanksgiving period determine the quality of a company's financial health.

At 8 a.m. on Black Friday 2004, Wal-Mart President Michael Duke, visiting an Atlanta store, realized that it was not as busy as he expected.[1] To understand the situation better, he visited local competitors. His observations, together with information he began receiving from around the country, convinced him that without quick action, Wal-Mart's holiday sales would be anemic. By afternoon, local and national managers had discussed markdowns that could improve customer counts. Even so, on Saturday Wal-Mart warned Wall Street of possible weak results.

Over the weekend, Wal-Mart's senior-most executives sharply discounted many prices. They also personally called their counterparts at key suppliers to ensure that they would be able to service any resultant surge in demand. Over the next fortnight, Wal-Mart changed advertising and merchandising and reduced prices further. Up to five hundred employees suggested immediate fixes at a town-hall meeting with management. In early January, Wal-Mart announced that its actions had enabled it to exceed the guidance it had given Wall Street.

Wal-Mart's actions during those two weeks were undoubtedly textbook examples of superb management. But did they measure up to the standards of an Adaptive Business? Did Wal-Mart intelligently and effortlessly adjust to major shifts in market conditions? Without a doubt it adjusted. The shift was also intelligent; before implementing its primary response (price cuts), its executives ensured that suppliers could honor the company's commitment to consumers.

But suppose Mr. Duke had not been in Atlanta. Would he have noticed that something was amiss as early as he did? Alternatively, suppose that because of local market conditions, the Atlanta store had experienced normal or better customer traffic. In a culture famous for an unwavering focus on meeting numbers, what would Mr. Duke's likely response have been to the *initial* reports of problems in some stores? We can be sure that Wal-Mart's awe-inspiring use of information technology would have, at some time that day, established the reality of a crisis. However, *it is unlikely that a junior manager in Atlanta would have been able to initiate a response.* Absent such an ability to deal with a *normal* business problem, a company cannot be considered able to *effortlessly* adjust in response to market changes. As such, judged solely on the basis of this incident, Wal-Mart's actions were merely effective crisis management and not a demonstration of adaptive capabilities.[2]

The situation at Nokia after the fire at Philips was very different. The production planner who first noticed the problem and initiated a response was simply doing his job. Indeed, Nokia actively designed his job to produce this outcome. Virtually all subsequent actions, including, for example, the move to more frequent monitoring of the situation, followed a script that had been put in place long before the fire.

I do not mean to suggest that there were no flared tempers or a sense of urgency. But the fire was "business as usual" internally. Tapio Markki, the first senior executive who heard of the fire, told me that top management's involvement was either an aberration (Pertti Korhonen) or fortuitous (CEO Jorma Ollila); normally, senior executives stayed informed but got involved only if asked:

> During the fire, what was an exception...was that top management, like [Mr. Korhonen], got involved so quickly. That made it bigger for outside people.... [Mr. Ollila] happened to be on his way back from the U.S., and so we had him meet Philips at the same time.

In all likelihood, the aberration stemmed from the newness of Nokia's adaptive capabilities. Mr. Markki himself had joined Nokia in 1997; most of his extensive prior experience had not been in supply chain or procurement. His boss, Vice President Jean-Francois Baril (currently Senior Vice President for Sourcing and Procurement for all of Nokia), had designed many of Nokia's policies but at that time had been with Nokia only fourteen months. So, Nokia's collaborative culture almost demanded Mr. Korhanen's involvement. Mr. Markki nicely summarized how Nokia's reaction today would differ from Wal-Mart's:

> When I learned of the fire, I was in a meeting, and I stopped it. If the fire happened today, I wouldn't stop my meeting, but we would *still* react rapidly. We are mostly able to sense and respond, as you call it.

The contrast between the two companies suggests the first Design Principle for adaptive companies: ***Embed sense-and-respond capabilities within normal plan-and-execute processes.***

The Importance of Being Earnestly Adaptive

Plan-and-execute processes deal with what is known and/or expected; sense-and-respond capabilities must address what is unknown and/or unexpected. Normal work processes and systems must enable people to do both. Absent such integration, people (and processes) may not be able to identify and address the unusual, unexpected, or spectacular as they execute the mundane. Such a disconnect may give rise to crises or missed opportunities. Well-managed companies may be able to react to these, but they won't be able to *proactively* exploit them.

I am far from the first to point out this limitation of a plan-and-execute approach; that credit belongs to Toyota's Taiichi Ohno. I summarize his brilliant insight from fifty years ago (1958) as: *Companies stumble when the sophistication of their planning outstrips the reality of their execution.* In 1958, most companies controlled supply-and-demand chains with Manufacturing Resource Planning (MRP). MRP began with forecasts of final product needs and progressively worked upstream, creating time-phased plans for execution. Mr. Ohno turned this logic on its head—upstream workgroups should do their work *only* on the basis of actual, observable demand from their downstream customers—and introduced Lean thinking to the world. In effect, he gave execution prominence over planning.

Sense-and-respond capabilities are a multidirectional generalization of Mr. Ohno's insight: Companies stumble when their planning-and-execution processes cannot match the pace with which changes propagate in a networked world. Businesses cannot simply rely on downstream execution to drive upstream work. They must be constantly vigilant for signals about actual events, wherever they may come from. At Nokia, the signal of the fire came from upstream supply markets. Elsewhere, they may come from adjacent product or geographic markets or even technology partners.

Embedding sense-and-respond capabilities within normal plan-and-execute processes is the modern-day equivalent of giving workers, not just masters, access to standard planes, micrometers, and engineering drawings. Doing so makes sensing and responding everyone's responsibility, not just that of the most senior people or dedicated groups of specialists. The magnitude of change needed should not be underestimated: the execution of work will be substantially transformed. Without such a change, no company can be adaptive.[3]

Managers' jobs also must change; at all levels, they must bear the primary responsibility of designing embedded sense-and-respond capabilities. Their efforts must focus on deciding what the company must sense, how it must do so, and how it must respond.

What Must the Company Sense?

For a while, my family lived in an apartment complex with hundreds of units. Generally very well managed, the complex had one terrible problem: the fire/smoke alarms in the units were so sensitive that no one could cook without setting them off. Even in Boston's freezing cold, we opened all windows and doors, aimed a fan at the sensor nearest the kitchen, and stood ready to wave a towel near the sensor. If the sensor's indicator began its dreaded red blink, within seconds, an ear-piercing screech would begin. The real estate company refused to adjust our alarms, so family members quickly unlearned a long-taught lesson: we stopped reacting to the screech by preparing to respond to possibly grave danger. We also paid no attention when alarms shrieked in neighboring apartments, even though we knew that if a fire broke out, it would spread rapidly.

This everyday story illustrates a clear guideline for designing sensing capabilities: *Clearly identify a handful of critical opportunities and challenges that must be sensed, and focus on these.* Executives cannot become overzealous and design sense-and-respond systems for every possible eventuality. If they do, their staff—and those of their partners—will simply ignore the incessant signals so that they can get their plan-and-execute work done.

An oxymoronic term, *predictable surprises*, coined by Michael Watkins and Max Bazerman, describes an almost perfect filter for focusing the company.[4] A predictable surprise is a problem with three characteristics: at least some people know that it exists; it is worsening with time; and, if unaddressed, it might become a crisis. (The explosive growth of airline frequent flyer miles is one of Mr. Watkins and

Mr. Bazerman's business-oriented examples. Each additional mile given is by itself innocuous. However, if an airline had to honor all the free flight commitments it had made one mile at a time, it would probably go bankrupt.)

To perfect its role as a filter, the definition of predictable surprises must be broadened in two ways. First, it must also cover opportunities that, if ignored, would not be exploitable. Such failures can be as deleterious for companies as incipient crises. Second, it must cover events that are predictable, not because they build up over time, but because they belong to *known groups of recurring problems or opportunities.* Any occurrence of such an event may be routine (predictable), but one could possibly provoke a crisis or create a huge opportunity (surprise). For example, consider the idea that "Customers make changes in their orders." One change might provoke an extended yawn. Another might be cause for reassessing retirement plans, if it took the form of a cancellation of a huge order after the company had expended irrecoverable resources to fulfill it.

Executives seeking to build sensing capabilities should review all such predictable surprises in order to identify which predictable surprises deserve a response, when, and how.

At Nokia, the disastrous experiences of 1995 focused attention on one predictable surprise: Some day, some time, some supplier would experience a catastrophic failure, and when that happened, Nokia would be very vulnerable. This was not a case of generals preparing to refight their last war. The intensity in Mr. Korhonen's voice was palpable when he told me:

> At that time, IT was booming. What did that mean? No suppliers had anything available. Bloody hell—no components, no suppliers! What do I do if I am short of 30 million flash memories or 100 million filters?
>
> The business situation we were in was all the time shortage of parts…because the business was booming and everyone was sending purchase orders for too much material. We had to

make sure that we had the sensing tools to make sure what was happening so that we could make our plans.

And so it was that although no one could have predicted that a fire would cripple Philips' New Mexico plant on March 17, 2000, Nokia had in place a system to sense such a possibility.

Companies have to identify their own predictable surprises based on their own particular situations. The categories of severe and/or frequent problems in Figure 2-1 might make for a good starting point for their search, but they should certainly not constrain the search. Moreover, it is important to recognize that as business conditions evolve, which predictable surprise should be sensed may change. Periodically, therefore, executives must reassess their business needs and refocus their sensing capabilities on the new criticalities.

Four Operational Sense-and-Respond Systems

Given the huge variety of possible predictable surprises, no single sense-and-respond system can serve as a universal prototype for all companies. To guide design efforts, I will pose a sequence of issues that executives must consider. To ground these issues in reality, I will first describe four sense-and-respond systems, including the one Nokia originally built.

Nokia's Plan Reconfirmation Process

Having determined what it needed to sense, Nokia turned to defining how it could do so. Mr. Korhonen said that the traditional managerial tools seemed inadequate for the purpose. Tools like MRP did not provide adequate feedback about what partners were capable of doing ("...it takes away transparency"). Lean tools like *kanbans* (in the form of purchase orders for each new shipment) sharply reduced the possibility of a corrective action ("Most companies—I'm really serious—send out a purchase order and expect that goods will show up on time and in the right quantity. When the goods don't arrive, they wonder what to do.").

So Nokia decided that it would *regularly and routinely* discuss its growth plans—which most companies consider confidential—with its partners. The discussions would cover immediate production needs, future volume changes, and anticipated new product and new technology introductions. Mr. Markki:

> ...we try to create long-term business pictures so that the suppliers have long-term visibility. [So] they can say, "With Nokia, the size of the business will be 200 million or 500 million next year."

The price the partners paid—there's always a price—for this information helped Nokia with both planning and sensing: *They had to confirm that they could fulfill the role assumed for them.* Would they have the necessary capacity? Would they be able to meet the planned delivery dates? Would they be able to support the launch? The shorter the horizon of the specific plans, the more often and more detailed was the information given and reconfirmation sought. If a partner couldn't agree to the original plan, Nokia would reconsider it. *If a partner ever failed to provide the required reconfirmation, Nokia would sense that it needed to take corrective action.* Mr. Korhonen:

> We were constantly communicating with our suppliers our plan. We asked them to confirm the plan to us, not individual purchase orders. "This is our new plan. Please confirm you can do this." In weekly meetings we review gaps. Whatever the gaps are against our plan, we start to [act].

Nokia did not stop with its own partners. To sense issues buried deeper in its network, it extended this same approach beyond them to their collaborators. It presented its plans directly to their senior executives and sought confirmations once a year. Subsequently, its staff conducted regular reconfirmation meetings. If they uncovered possible problems, they got Nokia's partners involved in the resolution efforts. On occasion, Nokia's partners too used its clout to resolve challenges they could not address on their own. How deep such efforts went into the broader network depended on the criticality of the issues involved.

When I first joined a consulting company, my boss taught me his fundamental rule for dealing with clients: "Ask, ask, ask, ask, ask!" In effect, Nokia turned repeated asking into a powerful sensing capability; it was literally that simple. *In doing so, it built the capability to sense into the day-to-day work performed by its people.* The capability was people-intensive and informal; Nokia staffers relied on the words and body language someone used to decide on a plan's viability or the need for a novel response. But it got the job done.

Yield Management with Sabre

Although it was developed for the airline industry, Sabre—and other similar services—is now used by many companies, including product-based ones, outside the travel industry.

American Airlines and IBM collaborated to create the first computer-based ticketing system. Sabre, the acronym for Semiautomatic Business Research Environment, became operational in 1960, and American Airlines spun it off as a separate company in 2000. In the intervening years, Sabre evolved to become one of the earliest—and most widely used—computer-based sense-and-respond systems ever created.

In 1976, American began installing Sabre terminals at U.S. travel agencies. Over the next decade, it expanded this effort into Canada and other key countries. Since travel agents found it easier to use Sabre than to handwrite tickets for other airlines, American rapidly expanded its market share. Other airlines were allowed to list their flights on Sabre in the late 1970s, but only after an antitrust investigation in the early 1980s did American's advantage get neutralized. In the meantime, over the vociferous objections of most airlines (including American), the U.S. Congress passed the Airline Deregulation

Act; the modern era of price competition began on January 1, 1983.[5] In 1985, American gave individuals with personal computers access to Sabre, making it a true distributed computer network. By 1988, individuals and companies could use Sabre to evaluate more than a billion fare options.

In the 1990s, as the present epoch emerged and computers became powerful, Sabre became capable of almost continually changing its listings. No longer did airlines have to work with relatively static, predictable determinants of seat demand (like the date or the day of the week). *They could now sense conditions*—such as the current competitive conditions and the demand for seats on a particular flight at a particular point in time. Based on such input, they could now *define their response*, which took the form of adjusting fares or releasing or limiting available seats. Where and when demand was high, prices shot up; occasionally, airlines lowered them to stimulate demand.

This sense-and-respond capability theoretically allowed the airlines to meet diverse customer needs. Practically, it allowed them to ensure a very high level of capacity utilization, a practice that came to be called "yield management."

The perfect market envisioned by economists since Adam Smith has become real. Prices respond to demand and no longer necessarily need any rational link to costs.

Hewlett-Packard's Buy-Sell Process

In contrast to the prior examples, HP's sense-and-respond capability is positively prosaic, because it is built into HP's materials-handling process. When it began outsourcing manufacturing in the mid-1990s, HP felt the need to conceal from its contract manufacturers the contractual terms it had negotiated with makers of components (like chips and DVD drives). This led it to create a process it calls "Buy-Sell."[6] Over the next decade, a process of experimentation led HP to build basic sense-and-respond capabilities into this process. This effort resulted from the insight that its more than sixty distinct product lines often share the same components.

The workgroup that runs Buy-Sell begins its job once customers (often retailers) have placed their orders and purchase and manufacturing contracts have been negotiated (often, but not always, as discussed in Chapter 5, "Succeed in a Dog-Eat-Dog World"). It consolidates the requirements of all the product lines to develop a complete picture of HP's needs.

Component makers deliver their wares, not to the contract manufacturers (as is the case for most other companies), but to one of three HP distribution centers (in China, Europe, and the U.S.). These centers supply the components on an as-needed basis to contract manufacturers. This avoidable step is inconsistent with the prevailing wisdom about world-class performance, because it adds assets and labor (and hence costs) to procurement. But it helps HP conceal its contractual terms and also enables it to sense and respond to real-time market and operational conditions.

The need to respond to real-time market conditions stems from the long and technologically irreducible lead times for many components. This fact forces HP to forecast sales and set purchase orders long before models of its more than sixty product lines appear on retailers' shelves. Karlheinz Hauber, a director in the Buy-Sell workgroup, told me that as demand patterns change, "...one (product line) may have parts it does not need, and others that need them may not." The distribution centers sense "...mismatches between what a retailer thought it would be able to sell and what it can" and respond appropriately. If demand for a model is low in a region, they first check to see if a different geographic region needs the product. If it doesn't, they check to see if the components can be used in other high-demand products. HP does "...thousands of such rebalancing across products a year."

Each distribution center, which serves several contract manufacturers, also can sense possible operational problems at component or contract manufacturers that could affect production and shipment. The centers do not physically segregate inventories in accordance with planned production by each manufacturer, but they do tag the inventory electronically. Because of the tags, unexpected changes in inventory levels immediately signal possible problems at specific manufacturers or suppliers. This system gives HP "...some time to react..." and provides it a "...trigger to escalate the problem."

Buy-Sell is prosaic, but that does not mean it is easy to create or manage on an ongoing basis. It requires an enormous level of sophistication not just in procurement and sourcing, but also in product development and information systems. Assuring interchangeability of components across models, geographies, and product lines requires careful coordination of work across multiple functions. This challenge gets complicated by the need to conceal contractual terms; in effect, at least some of the companies involved are not considered trusted partners.

Dell's Online Store

Founded in 1984, Dell took a mere eight years to become large enough to be included in the Fortune 500. Its fame did not lie in its products; right from its start, several of its competitors built sleeker, more powerful, more durable, more reliable computers. Rather, Dell created a unique business model: by conducting a direct online conversation with each consumer who logged on to its website, it could sell a personalized product that met the individual's needs.

At its best, Dell serves customers by weaving together several facets of its business. The ability to respond is defined long before a customer places an order; Dell's R&D staff designs its product to be extremely modular. Components can be swapped in and out at will so that the final product can accommodate chips of different speeds or hard drives of different capacities. The online storefront is very user-friendly so that it engages the consumer. It is tightly linked to the logistics, production, and supply networks so that Dell can actually deliver the orders it senses. Dell's analytical capabilities are very strong, allowing it to track and predict changes in market conditions and reposition products appropriately.

In reality, the system does operate like this, but over the medium term. In the short term, Dell senses and responds to customer needs when it can—and it shapes demand when it can't. Since electronic components have long lead times, if demand for a particular chip or screen type or memory type exceeds plans, Dell may not be able to respond. In such situations, it tries to get customers to change their minds. It features different systems more prominently in the online store. It raises the prices of the components and models that are in demand and lowers the prices of components and models it has in stock. In effect, at least some of the time, Dell does exactly what airlines and hotels do: it practices yield management, albeit at a level of sophistication that leaves many, if not most, customers satisfied.

How to Design Sense-and-Respond Capabilities

These four case studies suggest that there is no one-size-fits-all solution for the first Design Principle. Nokia and HP largely built supplier-facing capabilities, whereas American (which will serve as my proxy for all airlines and manufacturers using Sabre or similar capabilities) and Dell largely built customer-facing ones. As such, they focused on different issues and embedded their sense-and-respond capabilities into everyday work in their own ways. Their solutions undoubtedly arose from a series of trial-and-error decisions made over time. Even so, we can extract important lessons from their efforts.

Creating a Sensing Capability

Once executives use predictable surprises as filters to define what their companies must sense, they have to embed the sensing capability in plan-and-execute processes. They must decide what signals they should rely on, where the capability should reside, and how the sensing will happen. I will tackle the first two here and defer the last to later in the chapter.

The biggest challenge in determining what signals should be used to sense relevant predictable surprises is *noise*. Everything in nature varies randomly over time; this includes *all* measures used by businesses. This fact impedes the ability to ascertain when a specific change in the signal should trigger action and when it may be ignored. Good signals have one or both of two characteristics: they can be compared with clear benchmarks, and they appear—or fail to appear—repeatedly and consistently.

The signals at HP and American conformed to the first characteristic. Inventory levels can be compared to well-defined maxima or minima to assess market shifts. The number of seats sold by a certain deadline before departure can be compared to historical patterns to decide on price changes. The use of regular plan reconfirmation as a signal at Nokia conformed to the second characteristic. Mr. Korhonen told me that immediately after the Philips fire, despite Philips' initial belief that the problem was under control, the "...signal to do something" was that Nokia's inventory of chips was dropping and "We were not getting good confirmation..."

The next issue is whether the sensing capability should be embedded in the planning or executing processes (or both). This decision may determine a company's ability to assemble a satisfactory response. Typically, responding takes more time than sensing. So, capabilities built into a company's planning process tend to give it more time to respond than those built into the execution processes. Nokia and American based their sensing capabilities at the intersection of planning and execution, but leaning toward planning. HP based its sensing capability in execution, and this limited its options for reacting, particularly to real-time operational challenges.

So why would anyone choose the latter option? For two reasons: it may simply be impossible to do otherwise, and planning may be so temporally distant from execution that the signal emanating from there may not be useful. In HP's case, the long lead times for component delivery simply constrained its options.

Creating a Response Capability

Creating an effective response capability can be much more complex than creating an effective sensing capability. In all likelihood, *it will require substantial rethinking about how work is done.*

The design effort must begin with the predictable surprises that are critical. For each of these, executives must *assess how they would need to respond if the surprise actually occurred.* For Dell, it is entirely predictable that the demand for certain features may get triggered or suppressed by environmental factors outside its control. So, Dell needed capabilities to decide when and how much to change prices to shape demand, which alternative features should be pushed, and how further orders for components should be modified. For Nokia, the failure of a supplier would inevitably create component shortages. So Nokia needed capabilities to determine how it would reconfigure multiple product lines and possibly cannibalize one product line to protect another. Mr. Korhonen said that after the fire, Nokia had to find alternative components that were "close enough." To this end, it had to make changes to products and processes that were *not* directly affected by the fire and that it "...ended up optimizing the overall supply in the overall network."

Second, developers of response capabilities must identify the key bottlenecks, capabilities, weaknesses, or assets that could affect their ability to respond in their preferred manner. They have to ensure that these—production capacity, IT bandwidth, specialized skills, or even strategic partnerships—are available (at an acceptable cost!) if and when needed.

In Nokia's case, the possible need to reoptimize its products and processes in real time led to the identification of "people with the requisite skills and experience" as the absolutely critical resource. So, Mr. Korhonen noted, "Our purchasing people had to know the parts and products and components and people inside out so they could make the design changes." Mr. Markki added, "...we are trained to take the main role in responding, in determining how much we can do. What can the manufacturers produce? What can sales pull? What can R&D do to try to fix the technical issues?"

This understanding, reached in the 1990s, led Nokia to start changing the structure of people's jobs. For example, Mr. Markki said that procurement staff "gets involved" long before product development in creating the "development platform" that supports multiple products. He continued: "...we can even have influence of the design of one single component in a product. We have a bigger role if it is sole-sourced." On a regular basis, the procurement staff create with people in R&D and manufacturing "...different types of networks based on what we are trying to achieve."

Third, developers of response capabilities must *define how work will be coordinated when a predictable surprise materializes.* Organizations, like people, have habits that experts call "routines." Routines prescribe factors like the sequence, pace, and flow of work; behavior that is considered acceptable; who talks to whom, and when; and how information is created and used. Just as people fall into habitual patterns without thinking, so are routines "automatic," unconscious coordinators of normal work.

Routines for planning and executing are built over time. They become so embedded in companies that their very rationale is sometimes forgotten. To complement these, companies must build routines to tie together the activities needed to respond to predictable surprises. If not, people will not be able to act smoothly when they most need to do so.

Nokia created several routines for the possibility of supplier failure. Mr. Markki said that although Nokia didn't "...have a formal process of managing this kind of problem...," when such events occur, "...we all know what to do. I don't think anyone has said how to do it. It is learned practice, ...it is a natural practice." He went on to give a very specific and powerful example. While cross-functional teams of R&D, sales, and business people work on problems that are sensed, he said "...procurement and sourcing takes the central role." In effect, procurement seizes the reins without seeming to usurp power and provoking turf battles. It gives back the reins when the challenge has passed. This is seen as normal behavior—an accepted routine—at Nokia; in many other large companies, it would be unthinkable.

Finally, the designers must *evaluate when the company must actually act if it senses an opportunity or challenge*. This determination must be tackled last simply because it must take into account the tasks covered by the prior three responsibilities and determine the time needed to actually execute these in a specific instance. The designers must also account for their company's tolerance of risk: the lower the threshold, the earlier the company must act.

For HP, reconfiguring its product plan dynamically to match immediate market needs is not time-intensive or risky, so HP can prepare to act relatively late. For Nokia, reconfiguring the entire product line, manufacturing plans, and logistics worldwide would require a few stressful weeks. So, it had to be ready to go on alert as soon as the possibility of a problem was identified.

Considered together, the four guidelines just described lead to the inescapable conclusion that the cross-functional, cross-continental Nokia teams that swung into action after the fire were *not* crisis teams assembled on-the-fly. They cannot be compared to Wal-Mart's top managers personally calling their counterparts at supplier companies or organizing town-hall meetings. They did not typically create brilliant, novel solutions to the challenges they faced. Instead, they were parts of standing networks whose work had been redefined long before to deal with not just the mundane, but also the unusual and spectacular. Their executed response routines had been brilliantly embedded in normal plan-and-execute routines. Given the amounts of money at stake, perhaps they moved with great alacrity, but that is all.

The Role of Senior Executives

The discussion thus far may suggest to some that senior executives have no role to play in applying the Design Principle described in this chapter. That is not true; they must define the policy to guide these activities. There are four key reasons why. The first three are (equally) important in their own right. They also affect the fourth, which can raise Board-level issues.

Ensure That Multiple Sense-and-Respond Capabilities Are Coherent

In a typical large company, all facets of a complex sense-and-respond system will not fall magically into place at once. Solutions to perceived problems will be developed empirically over time through a process of trial and error. HP, for example, created the Buy-Sell process when it felt it was losing power to its contract manufacturers and discovered the sense-and-respond benefits over time. At Nokia, Mr. Korhonen acknowledged that at the outset, they "...had no idea what changes to make" and that "...there were many 'aha!' moments." Moreover, they "...didn't know before time how everything would look..." and, in effect, embarked on "...a learning journey."

Consequently, while senior executives will not actually be involved in the detailed design of sense-and-respond capabilities, they must ensure that various initiatives to create such capabilities across the company (at different points in time) are effectively coordinated. Sensing capabilities probably should not be duplicated. More importantly, response capabilities must be choreographed into smoothly functioning routines that do not confound each other's efforts.

Moreover, one cannot simply take "sense-and-respond capabilities" and set them down amidst existing "plan-and-execute capabilities." The designers have to look cross-functionally and cross-organizationally; their changes will affect people, organizational units, IT, and performance evaluation systems. Their mandate must go beyond traditional continuous-improvement efforts, Mr. Korhonen said:

> When the functional silos are there and you tell them to do continuous improvement, they will. But this means that they will dig the silo deeper and deeper. And now, to this, if you add an information system, what do you do? There I stand in the bunker and take the information system, and it is like putting cement in. And there we stand, cementing ourselves in. What we had to do was to subordinate functional goal and measures...

Bluntly stated, the political backing of senior executives is essential for addressing such coordination and potentially turf-related issues.

Determining the Role of Technology

This is, after all, the epoch triggered by distributed computer networks. Increasingly, sensing capabilities in particular will become highly reliant on technology. The critical issue here is that technology-driven sensing capabilities will increasingly challenge the traditional demarcations of company boundaries, raising important questions about governance structures.

The sense-and-respond systems of Nokia, American Airlines, HP, and Dell were effective even though the technologies implicit in them were not hugely sophisticated. In fact, I picked these examples to make this very point. Nevertheless, the truth is that the world has already moved well past these technologies. Even though Nokia used almost a paper-pen-phone-based sensing capability in 2000, today it works with an Internet-based network (RosettaNet) that enables automated transactions among businesses. It also is experimenting with radio frequency ID (RFID) tags that enable the sensing and tracking of goods flow. (Incidentally, the use of RFID is being aggressively championed in the U.S. by Wal-Mart and in Europe by Germany's Metro AG, which is the world's fifth-largest retailer.) And in some sense, even these emerging technologies are passé.

Academics and vendors are already testing "software agents" in laboratory (and select business) settings.[7] Very simplistically, these agents are bits of software that can "negotiate" routine, repeatable decisions (such as reordering supplies) with their counterparts in other companies on a sense-the-need-and-respond-to-it basis. Theoretically, agents cannot go beyond their terms of reference; they must refer exceptions to humans. But consider the implications of the conjunction of two well-understood statistical facts. The first states that even a process that is working "perfectly" (say, a Six Sigma process) will produce 3.4 errors per million opportunities. The second essentially states that any effort to reduce "false positives" will inevitably raise the probability of "false negatives" and *vice versa*. The first fact ensures that errors will occur even in a flawlessly operating system of software agents. The second fact ensures that all costs of these errors cannot be simultaneously eliminated. Together, they imply that *inevitably, sooner or later, a large, possibly huge, mistake will occur.*

This does not mean that we should not implement such sense-and-respond capabilities. It does mean that we should not undertake such implementations blindly. Some time ago, I asked the executives of several companies producing such tools, "Assuming this works, where will one company end and another begin? If an agent makes a billion-dollar mistake, who will be responsible? If an agent unwittingly involves a company in an illegal transaction, who will be responsible?" Far from giving coherent answers, most of the executives—leaders of small technology companies—did not even comprehend the issues.

This is the world into which CEOs and Boards must lead their companies. Unlike the creators of these technologies, top executives, CEOs, and Boards cannot afford to remain ignorant of the policies and legal ramifications of their use. They therefore *must* develop the policies within which their companies will use technology, or short-term gains will give rise to long-term pain.

Veering from Customer Intimacy to Being a Peeping Tom

Good customer-facing sense-and-respond capabilities inevitably raise important questions about privacy and ethics which, in many jurisdictions, will have major regulatory and legal implications. The emerging technologies will exacerbate these concerns, because they will give companies unprecedented powers. These powers could deliver great benefits to customers, companies, and society in general. However, whether they do so will depend on how companies use these powers and how positively societies regard their actions.

To understand why, consider American Airlines' sense-and-respond system. A cynic would say that American uses it to get customers to change their preferred travel plans or pay through their noses for their inability (or unwillingness) to do so. The system does not help the customers; it only improves American's profitability. Dell acts identically when it adjusts its prices to improve the relative attractiveness of computer models that are not popular. As a capitalist, I cannot help but applaud the efficacy of these business models. But cynical use of technology leaves many customers feeling manipulated. They may be able to do nothing more than gnash their teeth most of the time, but when they can, they may also turn on these companies. Certainly, the U.S. airline industry has lost the loyalty of its customers; virtually no customer shed a tear when, one by one, most of the big names—United, US Airways, Delta—had to turn to bankruptcy courts for protection.

The unwavering bias in creating sense-and-respond capabilities must be: First of all, do no harm, particularly in business-to-consumer interactions. *Approvals for all sense-and-respond capabilities should be to seek clear answers to two questions: Is it ethical? Could it adversely affect our brand image?* Senior executives should ensure that the pursuit of immediate profits does not end up hurting the company (and business in general) by attracting legal constraints to this capability.

Indeed, early efforts deploying RFID have already given rise to Orwellian fears. Organizations opposing its use are gaining traction in the media and with legislators.[8] Viviane Reding, the European Commissioner for Information Society and Media, warned that although RFID is important, it "also raises concerns about trust. If we don't remove the trust problem, well, then the business won't fly." The European Commission has already begun a public inquiry into RFID.[9] Any American who dismisses this story as European paranoia should pay attention to the fact that by mid-2005, *thirteen* American states had considered or were considering anti-RFID legislation.[10] In fall 2006, California Governor Arnold Schwarzenegger vetoed a bill (the Identity Information Protection Act of 2006) that the state's legislature had passed that proactively banned the use of RFID to track people.

The fact that thus far legislative efforts have failed is not important; the fact that restrictive legislations have been proposed even though these capabilities are nowhere near mass deployment *is*. Imagine the following scenario: A company whose general behavior is considered dubious by many exposes the medical or financial data of a large number of people to theft or fraud because of its inappropriate use of sense-and-respond capabilities. If this occurs, I suspect businesspeople, technologists, and academics would debate which saying best captures the moment: Walt Kelly's "We have met the enemy, and he is us" or Shakespeare's "The fault, dear Brutus, is not in our stars, But in ourselves..."

The Power to Reshape an Industry

In May 2002, I created and ran a conference for GlaxoSmithKline titled "Thriving in a World of Anywhere, Anytime Drug Distribution."[11] The attendees, all members of Glaxo's distribution channels, included about sixty senior vice presidents and vice presidents from huge wholesalers and retailers like McKesson, Cardinal, Wal-Mart, and CVS, and C-level executives from regional companies. Industry journals widely reported on the event.

I showed the attendees a photo of an AutoID chip—an RFID tag that is literally as small as a dust speck—and asked if it could affect their industry. "No," they said, uniformly. "Which illnesses would be curable/controllable if the correct dosages were taken on time?" I asked. AIDS, tuberculosis, and other scourges that could become drug-resistant because of noncompliance were mentioned. "Imagine," I said, "if we could track every single dose of medicine from the factory to the point and time of consumption with an AutoID chip. How would the practice of medicine change?" The room broke into an animated discussion of patient and societal benefits, which broadened into discussions about counterfeiting and other problems.

Later, I asked them whether in the not-too-distant future genome-based medication for Amit Mukherjee who lived in Massachusetts could differ slightly from the medication for an Amit Mukherjee who lived in California. Getting their assent, I asked, "How many of you have systems and processes to sense and distinguish between the demands from the two Amits?" No one did. "How many of you have the systems and processes to respond to the demands from the two Amits?" No one did. "How long would it take you to develop these?" After a lively discussion, they settled on an answer: about a decade. "So, how likely is the following scenario? One of these years, Glaxo's CEO—or the CEO of a competitor—will announce a new genome-based drug to Wall Street, and the share price will rise. Then, a few days later, he or she will admit that the company lacks the sense-and-respond capabilities to reliably deliver the drug to patients. The share price will collapse." The dominant answer? "Quite likely."

Later, we discussed nuts-and-bolts issues of sense and respond in the industry. How would work flow? Who would own the sensing system? Who would own the data? What current industry practices would impede its adoption? We also explored the lack of trust among the different segments of the pharmaceutical industry and the impact this would have on the resolution of these issues.

By late 2005, the pharmaceutical industry began addressing several of the issues we had discussed. Many distributors and retailers used to systematically buy larger quantities of drugs than they really needed, expecting the manufacturers to regularly raise their prices. Sense-and-respond technologies, combined with fears about regulatory action, eliminated this practice. This, in turn, had a major impact on the finances of the distributors. A senior vice president, whose company executives had attended the conference, told me about the knockdown, drag-out battle that was raging among some of the manufacturers, wholesalers, and retailers for control of the industry's emerging RFID capabilities. Who would control the data, which would be enormously valuable to many parties? At least one major consulting company, instead of advising its clients, had staked its own claim.

Just as sense and respond transformed the airline industry, so it will transform the pharmaceutical industry—and every other industry it touches.[12] Along the way, it will raise issues that can only be resolved well above the pay grades of most managers and staff. The most powerful systems will inevitably involve multiple players. Many will be partners, but just as many will be competitors. How a company positions itself among them will undoubtedly affect its fortunes. Enormous amounts of money—in the billions of dollars—will be at stake. Thousands of jobs will be on the line. Major societal benefits and associated ethical and legal issues have to be negotiated. Mid-tier managers and rank-and-file staff will play key roles in dealing with critical nuts-and-bolts issues, but they will need policy guidance from the top.

Companies in which senior executives shoulder this responsibility proactively will thrive. Companies in which they do not may flounder.

Why CPGCo Stumbled: An Inability to Sense and Respond

A very large, profitable, well-known consumer products company ("CPGCo") sold low-priced products in an industry that also had luxury items. Determined to change the company's positioning and foreseeing demand growth across all segments, CPGCo decided to go upscale. The raw materials for all CPGCo products were agricultural; the new products required far more customization and quality control than did the existing ones.

To support the product line expansion, CPGCo's Board made bold investments. It integrated backwards to give itself total control over better-quality raw materials. It redesigned its entire distribution chain and added new distribution centers. It also implemented a state-of-the-art production planning software package.

Chaos followed the smooth implementation of these initiatives. At a weekly meeting chaired by a senior, well-respected executive, market planners gave orders about what to produce and when to ship. Manufacturing managers then pronounced these orders dead on arrival.

CPGCo's supply-and-demand networks had became much more complex than in the past. Its new software certainly allowed it to develop plans for this complex market, but raw-materials maturity and product manufacturing remained unpredictable. Even with state-of-the art technology and science at its disposal, CPGCo, like all its competitors, could not predict precisely—and in line with the planning cycle—if all the raw materials that it needed for production would actually be available for use. Consequently, the attendees at the weekly meetings almost always had to scramble to adjust the plan manually—but this was difficult to do well. By the end of its peak selling season, repeated instances of ineffective planning not only cost the company significant revenues, but also left it holding a huge inventory of unneeded products.

CPGCo's Board and management were right to anticipate the need for better planning given all the changes they had introduced. However, they did not appreciate how important it would be to sense the latest raw-materials conditions and respond to these on-the-fly. So, they did not build the processes, tools, organizational structures, or even the culture that would enable CPGCo to sense and respond effectively. Nor did they create the capability to learn from their experiences.

So, You Are Not the CEO...

While writing this sidebar in the prior chapters, I focused on individual managers, because an individual cannot advocate for change if he or she has not objectively thought about his or her particular work environment. However, this chapter and some of the subsequent ones address what *groups of managers and professionals* should do if they want to apply the Design Principles:

1. Agree on the *criteria* for determining which predictable surprises *must* be addressed, because you will not have the time, resources, *and political clout* to do everything. Having this discussion before defining predictable surprises will help keep destructive politics out of the evaluation.

2. Search for predictable surprises (of both types) that are critical for your business. Figure 2-1 is a good starting point, but sticking with it is not enough.

3. Look for simple sensing capabilities that can actually be embedded in normal plan-and-execute work. The Lord Chancellor and the SPC charts changed the world not because they existed, but because good managers made their use easy. *An imperfect but usable system is better than a perfect, cumbersome one.*

4. Attempt to create the best response capabilities that do not need senior management approval. An imperfect system that middle management can activate is better than a perfect one

> that it cannot. It may not obviate a crisis, but if it reduces its magnitude, the company will be well ahead of the game.
>
> **5.** Wherever possible, rely on informal networks and relationships (rather than formal structures and processes) to execute the aforementioned tasks.

Endnotes

[1] The story reported here is summarized from "Before Christmas, Wal-Mart Was Stirring," by Tracie Rozhon, the *New York Times*, January 5, 2005.

[2] Wal-Mart is clearly a leader in applying the fourth Design Principle (regarding technology).

[3] In contrast, consider the many so-called Lean Sigma companies. They deploy "Six Sigma Black Belts" to drive improvement projects, but most do not routinely use the scientific approach that underpins Lean Sigma in *normal, day-to-day work*. Labels are not reality.

[4] *Predictable Surprises: The Disasters You Should Have Seen Coming*, by Max Bazerman and Michael Watkins, Boston: Harvard Business School Press, 2004.

[5] "What Prompted Airline Deregulation 20 Years Ago? What Were the Objectives of That Deregulation and How Were They Achieved?" by John W. Barnum, http://library.findlaw.com/1988/Sep/1/129304.html. Also see "Airline Deregulation Act" on Wikipedia, http://en.wikipedia.org/wiki/Airline_Deregulation_Act.

[6] I will mention only aspects of the Buy-Sell process that are relevant to creating sense-and-respond capabilities. Many business journals have extensive discussions of other features.

[7] For example, see http://en.wikipedia.org/wiki/Software_agent and http://www.cs.cmu.edu/~softagents/.

[8] "RFID: Big Brother in Your Pants?" *StateNet Capitol Journal*, July 4, 2005.

[9] "Supermarket fills aisles with RFID," by John Blau, *InfoWorld*, March 10, 2006.

[10] Ibid., *StateNet Capitol Journal*.

[11] At that time, I headed Forrester Research's strategy consulting group, which I had started. Several Forrester analysts participated in this conference.

[12] For another recent example, consider the impact that Netflix, partnering with the U.S. Postal Service, had on Blockbuster—or on your neighborhood video store. Or recall Frito-Lay's actions as a small, independent company decades ago. Frito-Lay created a simple, largely manual sense-and-respond system that assured every

mom-and-pop retailer in small towns and rural America a delivery of even the smallest order every time it needed one. Any operations researcher can prove that the cost of such a 100% service level system should bankrupt a company. Yet Frito-Lay thrived and reshaped the industry because retailers gave it almost all their shelf space.

5

Succeed in a Dog-Eat-Dog World

The early years of the twenty-first century have not been kind to the American automobile industry. The collective U.S. market share of the so-called Big Three dropped from 71.6% in 1990 to 58.6% in 2004 to 52% in 2006 to 48.1% in 2007.[1] Seemingly, the only way they can convince large numbers of Americans to buy their cars is by offering huge discounts that at best produce minimal to no profits and at worst, losses.

While there are some bright spots in overseas markets, the overall picture is very bleak. Ford is doing very well in Russia (and more generally in Europe), while General Motors has found encouragement in Latin America, Africa, and the Middle East.[2] Nevertheless, Toyota is poised to become the largest car maker in the world by 2009, when it is expected to produce almost 9% more cars than GM did in its best year ever (1978).[3] Looking further ahead, car makers from around the world are already actively competing in the potentially huge Indian market, which is soon expected to grow more rapidly than any other. In contrast, GM announced its *intention to enter* the market in early 2007, while Ford is said to be *studying* whether to compete with smaller cars.[4]

The industry is also going through substantial restructuring. Between 2000 and January 2006, the three companies collectively announced the elimination of 140,000 jobs, a third of their North American payroll.[5] Additionally, they embarked on restructuring efforts to cut their operating costs by billions. Their pain propagated through their network of suppliers. Delphi and Vistacon, which were once divisions of the auto giants, as well as independents like Dana, had to seek the protection of bankruptcy courts. Daimler ultimately gave up on its nine-year marriage to Chrysler. Having paid $36 billon in dowry, it sold Chrysler to the private equity firm Cerberus for $7.4 billion; most of the money did not come to Daimler. Indeed, some who have analyzed the deal say that Daimler actually paid Cerberus to take Chrysler off its hands.

Industry executives and many analysts have blamed labor costs for much of the industry's travails; nonunionized Toyota plants pay $20 to $30 (including all benefits) less per hour than do the American ones. Simply funding healthcare benefits promised to retired workers adds $1,500 to the cost of a typical American car.[6] The 2007 negotiations with the United Auto Workers union should eliminate the caterwauling about this challenge. GM's negotiations, for example, led to the formation of a trust fund that will eliminate, almost instantly, $55 billion of debt from its balance sheet—almost enough to restore one's faith in the tooth fairy!

What the recent negotiations have really done is taken away the excuses that shielded weak American management. (In rare candid moments, top industry executives admit to having built up an unsustainable bureaucracy over the years.[7, 8, 9]) As journalist and economist Ben Stein pointed out, *on a global basis*, Japanese auto workers are compensated only slightly less and Germans *more* than their American compatriots. Moreover, average labor costs are only about a tenth of the cost of a car or truck. So, he wrote, "It's not the workers' fault, even though they will be blamed for it because they are the punching bag at this point. It's management's fault."[10]

Now auto industry managers have to prove they can actually create cars that customers want to buy. They have done so off and on. Chrysler, which recently went through a mini-turnaround (before falling apart again), produced the Chrysler 300 sedan, which many consumers bought. GM's Cadillac Escalade also earned strong reviews. Many analysts, however, question whether the industry is up to doing so *consistently*.[11]

I am one of the skeptics, for I believe that even repeating the Chrysler 300 and Cadillac Escalade feats consistently will not be enough. While the former was good, it was only good enough to *reduce the discounts Chrysler offered to sell it from its fleet average of $3,760 to $900*.[12] Indeed, even glowing articles about Chrysler's achievements in 2006 used language that caused me to imagine the journalists typing their stories with their fingers crossed behind their backs.[13]

The industry must do much more. Its ticket to play must be the development of the intestinal fortitude needed to make big bets on technology and infrastructure that *might* pay off after many years. Toyota started working on hybrid engines for the twenty-first century car in 1994.[14] Sooner or later, because of the European End of Vehicle Life Directive and rapidly rising concerns about global warming, Americans will have to make many such bets.

Much more importantly, the U.S. auto industry must change its behavior towards its partners who build markets, create technologies, assure supply, and develop complementary resources. Too often today the industry's attitude toward potential and actual partners is arrogant and ruthless. Such behavior does not recognize that the blurring of industry boundaries and the fragmentation of work have taken away its power to control its own destiny. To create a winning stream of products and technologies, it will have to rely heavily on others who are at least as powerful. For example, over the last decade, the electronics industry has become a critical collaborator; the success or failure of many a car or technology is already dependent on the performance of its electronics. In the years ahead, the industry will not be able to make the gutsy bets it needs to without the unstinting support of others.

Under the circumstances, the industry's strategic behavior, not just costs, needs radical restructuring. If it fails to appreciate this, in the next few years the only bragging rights its executives will have is to shout from the rooftops, "We haven't been swept into Lake Michigan—yet!" Of the four Design Principles for Adaptive Businesses, the one this industry needs to adopt the most—not just to succeed, but merely to survive—is the second one: ***Adopt strategies that promote collaborative action among network partners.***

A Dog-Eat-Dog World

Not too long ago, the top executive of a component supplier ("AutoCo") asked me to audit its American manufacturing operations. When I met with the management team, the stark reality of their world hit me in the face. Though nowhere near best in class, the plants were well managed. The harried executives were struggling to reduce costs as much as they could. Chinese manufacturers posed an immense threat, for they could cheaply produce many of AutoCo's products.

AutoCo executives felt that they produced higher-quality products and that they responded better to their customers' needs, but these abilities did not win them business. They said that the largest domestic auto parts makers simply handed over their designs to the Chinese, who offered to make them at lower costs. The parts makers then asked AutoCo to match those costs—without reducing quality or delivery levels to those of the Chinese—or lose their business.

What about your patents, I asked? Weak smiles and disbelieving shakes of heads followed as they digested my naïveté. Patents, they said, meant nothing; despite these, the business would go overseas. But if the Chinese couldn't perform, wouldn't AutoCo gain some leverage? Weak smiles and disbelieving shakes of heads followed again. ("This is the guy who is supposed to evaluate us?") Any attempt to exercise such leverage would lead to retaliatory action against the other product lines they sold to the same customers.

How did AutoCo come to be treated this way? Some may say that the American auto industry's harsh treatment of employees and suppliers dates back to the union-busting days of Henry Ford. I do not know whether that ancient history is relevant. The answer definitely dates to the mid-1990s, when—as the turmoil of epochal change began building up—GM appointed José Ignacio López de Arriortúa as its head of purchasing. As the Thunderbird Business School case "José Ignacio López de Arriortúa" documents[15], under Mr. López, General Motors began displaying an unprecedented degree of ruthlessness in its dealings with suppliers. In Toyota's version of Lean Enterprise, if Toyota engineers found cost improvements at a supplier, the supplier got to keep 30%-40% of the savings; GM confiscated all. Moreover, Mr. López reportedly tore up existing contracts and demanded new bids with huge price reductions, asserting that the suppliers would be bankrupt before courts of law could came to their aid.

I asked AutoCo's managers how they dealt with their customers' appalling behavior. They became quiet and looked at their boss. After a while, the boss said that they took their new ideas first to European and Asian customers, who treated them better. He then took me to see a section of one of the plants where AutoCo had invested heavily in new machines, infrastructure, and training to gear up production on a new product that would give its customer a small competitive edge. The long-term impact of actions like those that GM encouraged with its appointment of Mr. López is the loss of competitiveness in the U.S. auto industry.

AutoCo is not alone in the steps it took. "RevCo" used to operate under contracts with the U.S. car manufacturers and provided reverse-logistics services to their dealers. When a dealer had to make a repair under warranty, RevCo provided the replacement part and took back the defective one to harvest its components or repair it for future use in another vehicle. Because of its years of experience in looking at problematic parts, it had built a knowledge base that auto manufacturers should have considered far more valuable than the actual service it provided: *It understood, perhaps better than the people who had created the original products, how and why they were failing*. By tracking the pattern of incoming defective parts, it could warn the automakers of possible problems in their designs or manufacturing. In other words, *RevCo could provide an effective, operational customer-facing product and technology-focused sense-and-respond capability*. Yet, its efforts to market this knowledge to these companies generated reactions ranging from complete indifference to outrage that RevCo expected *any* payment for its service.

But knowledge is an interesting thing. Regardless of whether its creation takes massive amounts of time, energy, and resources or the brilliant insight of one or more great minds, knowledge may be hard to decode, decipher, and use without the active support of those who create and/or possess it. By acts of omission (suppressing key information) or commission (providing misleading information), those who create/possess knowledge can thwart its effective use by those who choose to appropriate it.[16] RevCo's customers could throw as many tantrums as they wanted, but they could not usurp its knowledge. They could retaliate by giving some or all of the reverse-logistics business to another provider or bring it in-house, but it would be a while before the new providers (if they were really good) would possibly be able to deliver similar insights as could RevCo. In the meantime, the opportunity to improve would be wasted.

Dissatisfied with the financial returns from its American customers, RevCo began focusing on Asian companies. It also began offering similar services to other industries. Ultimately, RevCo did not suffer; the same cannot be said of its American customers.

Why Companies Act Against Their Own Best Interests

While the destructive behavior just described is extreme, to a greater or lesser extent, the underlying issues can be observed in many business situations. Relationships between companies are often governed by assertions such as "If we tell them what our true inventory levels are, they will take advantage of us," "If we tell them that there's a better way of doing this, we won't get to keep a fair share of the savings," "We won't send our best engineers into this joint venture, because no one else will," and "Gimme five! I wrung another half-percent out of them!"

A game theory model called the Prisoner's Dilemma elucidates why companies behave like this. It has been widely applied in fields ranging from economic theory to Cold War military strategy. Its basic formulation should be familiar to anyone who watches (American) TV crime shows. The police arrest two suspects against whom they have weak cases and hold them in separate cells. They promise each leniency for implicating the other and harsh treatment otherwise. The prisoners do not realize that the threat is empty, but, unable to communicate with each other and concerned about being double-crossed, each one concludes that *regardless of what the other does,* he or she will draw a lesser sentence by implicating the other. Each then *makes a perfectly rational decision* to do so; jointly they give the police the ability to convict both.

The Prisoner's Dilemma is played repeatedly in business; companies working together individually make rational decisions that collectively produce bad outcomes. They do not convey their true inventory levels and experience the so-called "bullwhip effect." They don't tell their customer the better way of doing a job, and both see the business shift to an overseas company that has a lower cost structure. They don't send their best engineers into a joint venture, and then they wonder why it failed. They don't let their suppliers earn reasonable profits, and then they wonder why their competitor gets preferential access to a new technology. In each situation, the decision is rational. Extra inventory provides a buffer in tough markets. Not telling the customer the better way protects today's margins. Not sending the best engineers protects the base business. Extracting the last cent from a supplier improves today's profitability. Yet each decision hurts both parties.

Companies fall into the Prisoner's Dilemma trap because their people lack critical information about the consequences of their decisions. Patrick Scholler, an HP director, said the following when referring to a multibillion-dollar, multiyear components deal that HP had signed:

> ...how do you know you have a good deal? ...how do you *know* [that the deal terms you got] are the *best* over a multiyear period? You *can't*; it is not a question of being tough in the negotiation.

"You can't" know because often the governing factors are simply unknowable. HP's negotiator would not know in advance the precise volumes that HP would actually need (as opposed to what it expected to need), the market price that would prevail when it actually had to place a purchase order, and the total level of supply that would be available in the market at that time. After all, a ten-minute fire at a supplier could compromise the worldwide supply! Faced with the seemingly unknowable, companies focus solely on what they can. The buyer tries to beat down the supplier, and the supplier tries to extract the highest possible price from the buyer. Traditionally, Mr. Scholler said, HP took its "toughest negotiator" and "...put him in front of the supplier...to get you the best terms."

The problem created by the lack of knowledge gets exacerbated by people's concern that they could get blamed for how the future might evolve. In purchase negotiations, for example, a common challenge is the setting of maximum ("ceiling") and minimum ("floor") prices that would get paid under various conditions. Referring to these, Mr. Scholler continued:

> We asked people, "If statistics prove that in 80% of the cases you win and in 20% of the cases you lose, would you play?" Most people...said, "No, I won't play, because if I fail in the 20%, I may lose my job." In the case of a floor-protecting

supplier, it may mean paying a higher price than market for a given occurrence. No one wants to explain that to his boss...even though over time it is a very sound deal in HP's favor.

Pertti Korhonen summarized Mr. Scholler's analysis with a simple assertion: "It goes to fear." Because they "...don't know that they don't know," people default to following traditional negotiating practices unquestioningly and get pushed toward ruthlessness:

Conventional [wisdom] doesn't go far in acknowledging interdependency, trust, and giving control of your future to the other party. Conventional [wisdom] is about super-competitiveness.

And so, acting rationally, each party creates for itself a prison from which it cannot escape. The distrust between the parties renders them incapable of working collaboratively to create a solution that benefits both.

The Importance of Playing Nice

From the perspective of Adam Smith's invisible hand, a win-lose perspective would not matter if the work done by a company's partners were incidental to its performance. But that is not the case today. On the one hand, electronics and software have made most (but not all) products more complex.[17] This has happened despite concerted efforts to make products modular so that components produced by different workgroups can be assembled like Legos. For example, a top-of-the-line Mercedes S-class has about seventy "electronic control units," and a low-end Volkswagen Golf has about forty, to coordinate various mechanical systems.[18] This fact has made even companies like Mercedes, Toyota, and BMW susceptible to problems, including product recalls.[19] On the other hand, the decomposition of work has fragmented the information required to identify and resolve problems. The observer of a problem might not even know questions to ask of a counterpart halfway across the world where the problem might have originated. This raises the likelihood that undesirable incidents will occur—or incipient opportunities will pass by—before root causes are identified and resolved.

So, firms will increasingly find it impossible to sense a possible problem or opportunity and respond to it effectively without the goodwill of their partners. Stated differently, they will find it difficult to adopt Design Principle 1 if they fail to adopt Design Principle 2. You cannot cudgel a supplier into submission on issues when you choose to and then expect it to be helpful in sensing and responding when you feel you need help.

In the SAP survey of North American manufacturers, 73% of the respondents said that they were collaborating more or much more with their trading partners, and 79% were focusing more or much more on increasing their suppliers' participation in, and responsiveness to, their work. Strong pluralities of the interviewees also acknowledged the benefits of collaborating with peers and partners, as shown in Figure 5-1. They saw the biggest benefits in "improving product quality and performance" and "getting new products to market faster." (This is natural, because most companies track these dimensions of performance most closely.)

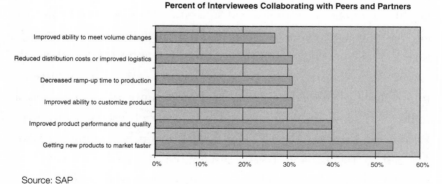

Percent of Interviewees Collaborating with Peers and Partners

Source: SAP

Figure 5-1   Benefits perceived from collaborating with peers and partners.

Although the American auto industry does not seem to share this belief, it is not immune to the necessity to collaborate, and has not been for a long time. University of Tokyo Professor Takahiro Fujimoto is an expert on the world auto industry.[20] I asked him what proportion of a typical car is designed and/or manufactured by companies other than the company whose name appears on the car. Mr. Fujimoto noted that in the late 1980s, car makers "outsourced" about *40% of the engineering*. He added, "We have not done detailed calculation since then, but this number seems to be higher now.... As for *manufacturing*, typical outsourcing ratio was about *70% in Japan*. It is a bit lower in Europe and America (before separating Delphi and Visteon)."[21] It would seem, then, that in this industry, creating bad blood with network members would be foolish at best and sabotaging oneself at worst.

Playing Nice—to Win

A more sophisticated version of the Prisoner's Dilemma ("multi-period Prisoner's Dilemma") assumes that the two suspects know that they might find themselves in police custody an indeterminate number of times in the future. Under these conditions, each suspect realizes that if he or she double-crosses his or her partner, the partner will do the same in the future. However, if each keeps quiet, the police must release them both. Thus, both suspects keep quiet. Each such occurrence increases each person's confidence in the other's (future) good behavior.

The implication of this model is clear: if people interact (work) with each other rationally and repeatedly, they should keep their partners' best interests in mind—not as an act of altruism, but one of enlightened self-interest.

Both Nokia and HP reached this conclusion and developed their own approaches to its implementation. As in the case of the first Design Principle, HP's approach, championed by mid-level managers, is formal; it is anchored on homegrown software. Nokia's approach is far more informal; its credence comes from its being advocated by top executives.

The PRM Program at Hewlett-Packard

About the time that Ericsson was scrounging for chips, HP also felt compelled to secure chips by agreeing to a multibillion-dollar multiyear contract. The negotiations had been effected in the normal "get the best deal" fashion. Corey Billington, a former HP vice president who is now a professor at IMD, wondered whether the contract had indeed produced a good outcome. The job of finding the answer serendipitously fell to Venu Nagali, a Ph.D. in mechanical engineering who at that time was a junior consultant to HP. (He currently holds the coveted title of Distinguished Technologist at HP.) Soon after taking on the task, Mr. Nagali had a "eureka moment":

> In most situations, the burden of bearing the uncertainty finally falls on the guy who is the weakest, because he cannot negotiate the risk.... If you look at conflicts between manufacturers and suppliers, you will find that there are ten cases of the suppliers getting dumped for every case of a supplier dumping a manufacturer.... I realized that we need to reduce the risk to suppliers. More generally, we need to pay the person who bears the risk. If we do so, over a period of time, both parties will win.

Mr. Nagali's insight, which should seem familiar to any student of finance, became the basis of HP's Procurement Risk Management (PRM) program. PRM introduced HP to the second Design Principle; it is currently used across roughly a third of HP's businesses. Importantly, it does not depend on the relative sizes of the negotiating parties; indeed, HP had felt itself victimized in the chip deal. Similarly, companies as large as Procter & Gamble and Unilever often feel significant pressure when dealing with Wal-Mart.

The PRM program first estimates quantities of components—memory sets, microprocessor chips, flat screens, DVD players—that HP will need.[22, 23] It then quantifies uncertainties in price, volume, and market availability in order to assess the level of risk it may face. Finally, the PRM software generates a range of options for HP executives to consider. At this point, a senior executive—whose level depends on the scope or criticality of the business—initiates conversations with a comparably senior executive at the supplier. The HP executive presents data on the full extent of the business relationship between the companies—including the high and low points of the prior year—to his or her counterpart.

Finally, the executive asks what information about their mutual dealings would make it easier for the supplier to run its business better. The options that PRM specifies for HP allow the executive to provide some or all of the information that the supplier needs to improve its own business. Eric Schneider, the vice president responsible for HP's mainline server business, became one of the first to adopt the program. He gave a simple example:

> When you are introducing a new technology or a new product, it is the riskiest time to estimate demand. Therefore, you need supplier flexibility. When it is the most difficult to forecast, you have to say, "I know this product is going to take off, but I can't forecast the exact timing. I will promise to buy a fixed amount from you. In exchange, you must promise to accelerate production if I need it—if things go better than expected." The interest they have is that they don't want to get yelled at by their bosses for having too much inventory or capacity. *By talking about our interests, we're better able to do this.*

"This" is achieve a mutually beneficial outcome. PRM does not eliminate negotiation, but it sharply reduces the likelihood that the negotiations will degenerate into a win-lose battle. Both parties see their perceived risks decline, sometimes substantially. In Mr. Schneider's example, the supplier can use the information confidently to make critical decisions such as whether it needs additional capacity. HP benefits by being assured that its partner will be ready with supplies as and when it needs them.

Risk attracts a premium, and its certain reduction reduces it. The lowered risk in this case gives *both* parties financial benefits. HP's own share of the savings—estimated to be over $100 million by 2004—continues to rise as new business units and their suppliers adopt PRM.[24]

There is, of course, no free lunch. Once commitments are given and formalized into a contract, both parties must honor them. This means, for example, that *HP sometimes buys components and commodities it does not need because of changed business conditions.* The description of Buy-Sell in Chapter 4, "Transform Everyday Work," alluded to this. Moreover, Mr. Scholler's discussion (in this chapter) of the difficulty of convincing people to move to win-win is also based on the making of such commitments.

Another benefit of PRM not only dwarfs the value of prices and flexibility so negotiated, but also truly captures the essence of the second Design Principle. In articles on PRM in professional journals, this benefit is inevitably not quantified and is described by the pedestrian term *assurance of service.* Yet, given how the financial markets react to network problems, it should warm the hearts of CEOs and CFOs. Mr. Nagali:

> What happens when something goes wrong and all contingency plans evaporate? ...At this point, you have two options. One, you can enforce a penalty. This is the lose-lose option. Two, you can ensure that when the supplier recovers, you get first dibs on the output. PRM takes us down the path of the second option. We had a situation where a supplier had a major shutdown. When it recovered, they met our demand for the previous month and for the current month before anyone else was given anything.

In a networked world, if the flow of goods gets disrupted, even temporarily, at one company, flows are affected throughout the network. Because Company A cannot give Company B what it needs, Company C, also a supplier to Company B and an innocent bystander, has to stop shipping to Company B. In such a world, a relationship that assures priority access can be invaluable. It takes win-win thinking out of the realm of altruistic behavior and into the realm of drivers of competitive advantage.

A Win-Win Policy at Nokia

In 1999, Mr. Korhonen added global procurement to his responsibilities for supply chain and manufacturing. This area had worked hard for many years to convince its external partners of the viability of the mobile phone business. "Nobody believed in the beginning how big this business would be," he told me. As such, Nokia had to "...persuade people to take risks, make major investments for us." To do so, Nokia "...behaved differently from many other companies." Mr. Korhonen:

> ...we were not buyers, we were sellers—of our business. We had to convince suppliers to give us what we needed. It forced us to create the concept of win-win.... But we had not institutionalized this.

To strengthen Nokia's capabilities, Mr. Korhonen convinced a Frenchman, Jean-Francois Baril, to join Nokia. Mr. Baril, who had, for the best part of fifteen years, managed procurement in two American companies, told me that Mr. Korhonen gave him the mandate to "...build the best sourcing and procurement program in the world."

Long before Mr. Nagali's "eureka moment," Mr. Baril had formed a similar jaundiced view of traditional intercorporate relationships. He gave me an example:

80% of the companies which are trying to implement Just-in-Time fail because they are just focusing their own interest into this process.... Big companies actually want to transfer the burden for the inventory on the smaller guy, and the smaller guy wants to transfer the burden on to an even smaller guy, and so on. What has happened if I work in this way? I've not brought any value into the overall system. I have just transferred the burden but not created any extra value or synergy.

However, his solution differed greatly from Mr. Nagali's. Passionate in his belief that "soft skills are very often taboo or forgotten in the business environment" but are "the basis of the new era of business," he simply decreed a policy of win-win. He asked me, "If you don't want my good thing and I don't want your good thing, how do I get to 1 + 1 = 3?"

Mr. Baril instructed his staff to search for the best outcome for all partners, not just Nokia alone. Nokia staff met with their counterparts in other companies. They talked at length about Nokia's long-term plans and the role that Nokia wanted the partner to play in those plans. They stated what Nokia needed and listened to their partners' ideas, needs, and objections. Each side provided its rationale for its views and supported it with as much information as it needed to reach a mutually acceptable deal.

Without a formal HP-like system, however, Nokia lacks a formal mechanism to compensate its partners if unanticipated changes in its plans cause them difficulties. When these occur, it looks for situation-specific ways to compensate them. For example, Tapio Markki said:

First of all, we don't have any firm process. In practice, we do it to a certain extent with suppliers with whom we deal with a lot.... We communicate how much capacity that we may use or not use as we get closer to the date. And there is a cost assumption with it.... They use "open book cost modeling" if we don't use the capacity. The suppliers modify some direct cost factors, and we pay that.

When I asked Nokia executives about the benefits of their policy, they did not focus on monetary outcomes, but described how their interactions with their partners changed over time, benefiting both parties. Mr. Korhonen gave one example: Nokia gets preferential treatment from key partners "...whether it is about new technology or allocation or adaptation to a major change in plans." Mr. Markki gave another, referring to the 2000 fire, noting that the changed interactions opened the option of moving some production to other Philips plants:

> One reason why we managed pretty well...was we were helping them to lever their production planning. It was eye-opening for them to see how we were helping them with once-a-week planning as opposed to the once-a-quarter they were used to before the fire. So they changed to conform at different stages of the process.

Implementing the Second Design Principle

The mathematical formulation of the multiperiod Prisoner's Dilemma produces a win-win solution solely because both suspects expect to interact with each other an *undetermined* number of times in the future. Were the number of interactions that would "end the game" fixed and known, each suspect would feel the pressure to incriminate the other during the last period of the game, making it the equivalent of the single-period game. This unraveling would lead to a domino effect of similar win-lose decisions in every earlier period.

In the business world, many events can "end the game." A change in the business cycle could shift power for several years from one segment of an industry to another. A manager could reach the end of his or her tenure in a position. People in such situations may either feel real pressure to defect or fear that their partner will and act to "protect" himself. As such, a win-win relationship could move to win-lose to lose-lose very quickly. HP's Mr. Schneider acknowledged that "...the PRM arguments will fail if someone doesn't keep the promise. I *have to* determine that I'll take the material if I guessed wrong." However, with a touch of surprise, Mr. Nagali noted, "Only in about 1% of the cases, when someone is down, commitments haven't been kept." Mr. Baril described a similar evolution of attitudes at Nokia:

> When I joined Nokia, it was very much the sellers' market. I was on my knees to get enough components to build our phones. After the dot-com bubble burst, market reversed, and for many people it would have been easier to operate in a less cooperative, more transactional way.... Some of my colleagues came to me and were questioning if the partnership way was the right way. I convinced them to continue with the win-win approach. *Today, it is in Nokia's genes.*

Getting to this point requires significant, concerted effort, for companies that want to do so must overcome the twin challenges of lack of knowledge and fear of criticism, described early in this chapter. Mr. Korhonen characterized it as, "It is about trust, about taking risks.... This requires a different level of maturity." How does a company get to this "different level of maturity"? The efforts of both companies provide a handful of important lessons.

First, Recruit Passionate Believers

Game theorists have established that it is possible to evolve to win-win even in situations where the predominant perspective is win-lose. *What is essential is a critical mass of people who believe in win-win.* These people search out others who share their beliefs, if they have the flexibility to do so. By working with each other repeatedly, over time they (as a group) outperform those with a win-lose mind-set. Their superior performance attracts the attention of others, who then join the group to gain the same benefits.[25] So, to get the process started, a company must focus on the true believers.

At Nokia, Mr. Baril was such a person. Sitting across from him in a small conference room in Palo Alto, I was mesmerized by his ardent, articulate advocacy:

> My baby is passion and trust.... A lot of business schools are focusing on the hard skills. But think about this. When you go to the Olympic games, the issue is not *only* hard skills. *Everyone* has them. The issue is about intense passion. Passion creates energy.... Why is Nokia better than any other company? It is the combination of the hard skills with soft skills, the collaboration and the partnerships both inside and outside the company.

"The bias towards win-lose," Mr. Baril said, "is the most difficult thing to unwire." True believers are needed to make this possible, because *they are willing to do the unusual, the unconventional, for win-win to gain a beachhead.* Someone who is concerned about how he or she will be viewed by others may not take such steps.

At HP, Mr. Nagali set up his team like a "stand-alone startup company" that was "always fighting for survival." His boss, Mr. Scholler, confirmed that instead of continuing to build its math skills, Mr. Nagali's team decided that "...at the end of the day, it is a sell, sell, sell job." To this end, the team began carefully selecting business units with which they would work. Mr. Nagali:

> ...We picked business units to target on the basis of whether there was a leading-edge executive who wanted to be among the first to try out a disruptive idea. We stayed away from most of the others who said, "I don't want to be a guinea pig." We decided that we've got to build up successful case studies before we approached [others].

With each such business unit, Mr. Nagali's team, which works as internal consultants, spent significant energy teaching the methodology, helping implement the capability, and catalyzing changes in their interactions with suppliers.

In Nokia's nonhierarchical culture, Mr. Baril had to go much further. Despite Nokia's long-standing bias toward win-win, initially his staff strongly resisted his breaking new ground by making win-win an official policy. Dispirited by the resistance, he considered resigning shortly after joining; Mr. Korhonen talked him out of doing so. Mr. Baril finally convinced his team with help from a renowned Finnish philosopher (and professor at the Helsinki Institute of Technology), Esa Saarinen:

> We were on this island in the middle of the sea.... All it had was a sauna. And Esa arrived on a speedboat in his legendary leopard jacket...and I wondered if the people would think that I was mad on top of having crazy ideas. But Esa was very respected in Finland and...agreed with my ideas. I hoped my staff would say, "I trust this guy, and so maybe it is worth it for me to try to understand what [Mr. Baril] is trying to do."

Nokia followed this off-site meeting with a focused effort to modify people's behavior. Externally, it organized seminars about itself, its plans, and its anticipated needs. It invited not just executives of its partner companies, but also rank-and-file staff who made decisions about whom to provide product, when, and why. Internally, it trained its staff, often on very basic issues about building strong relationships with people in other companies. Mr. Korhonen:

> ...when you have a problem, do you go to the supplier? Or do you ask the supplier to come to you, and you yell at them? Most of the time, we go to the supplier, or meet at some nice place offsite and spend some time together—perhaps in a sauna.

Focus on Solving Specific Practical Problems

Even with true believers leading the charge, companies should address immediate, practical issues of substantial value instead of initiating a crusade to change the world. Once people are convinced that win-win helps them in areas they care about, they become amenable to considering that by moving out of their comfort zones, they may create even greater value. For example, the PRM team often stayed away from seeking equitable risk-sharing or even assurance of supply when they engaged a new business unit. Mr. Nagali:

> The first VP we sold a [comprehensive PRM program] to—we pitched him for cost reduction. We always looked for a burning problem which made the executive open to any idea to fix the problem. So a burning problem and willingness to place bets. That was crucial. We made him successful, and without that, we would not have got executive visibility.

Nokia let the benefits of win-win become apparent to recalcitrant customers instead of pushing them into relationships they did not desire. Mr. Korhonen:

> ...very often we get changed orders because a competitor cannot deliver on an order. After having squeezed us on price and having gone to the competitor because of a better price, they come and ask us, "Can you help?" We help if we can. And maybe, for the next time, there is a little less squeezing on price. After operating like this year after year, they learn it is not about spot deals—that is not the way to add value.

Define Policies That Facilitate Information Sharing

It is impossible to develop a win-win relationship with others without sharing critical information with them. *Having* critical information is of little value unless it can be shared with those who need it to make key decisions. When we met, Mr. Korhonen stood up and acted as if he were cradling an infant whom he was trying to protect from prying eyes. He said:

> It gets really tricky. Possessing information becomes power. Without an attitude of win-win, there cannot be true transparency, and so, no information transfer. You end up making decisions with incomplete information. This ends up hurting both parties.

At HP, Mr. Nagali argued that lack of adequate information raised uncertainty and forced companies to bear "invisible costs." For suppliers, these costs were associated with issues that ranged from the size of customer orders to the size of factories. HP, he said, shares a lot:

> We tell them what demands we will make on them in the short term, the medium term, and the long term. Just that information makes their decision-making better.

However, no company can tell all outsiders everything! The key question, then, is *Who is authorized to share what information, with whom, and under what conditions?* I don't believe there is a "one size fits all" answer. At HP, which is famously decentralized, the senior executive dealing with a partner has all the relevant information and makes a case-by-case decision about what to share. Nokia, which is far more centralized, has broad policies based on a partner's importance. Mr. Markki estimated that in 2006, Nokia was "sharing everything" with "only five companies" and "sharing enough information" with twelve to fifteen more.

Sooner or later, senior executives must develop policies to govern information sharing. Nokia's and HP's approaches offer two polar models executives can emulate. Even in these cases, they have to decide, for example, what "sharing everything" or "sharing enough information" means. Until they do so, most managers will probably be overly cautious and share less information than they could or should. As a result, their companies will be less able to sense and respond or achieve win-win solutions than would otherwise have been the case.

Change the Metrics

In the case of AutoCo and RevCo, the American auto companies engendered win-lose behavior by not ascribing much value to innovation, quality, or service. More generally, if either party in a relationship fails to define success broadly, win-win solutions will not arise naturally and, indeed, relationships will degenerate into a win-lose battle.

The party that finds itself on the losing end will, if it can, protect itself by searching for victories in ways that are not subject to the negotiated contract. The results so obtained may not be pleasant for either party.

Consider again an example from Chapter 4: airlines lose their customers' sympathy by manipulating their sense-and-respond capabilities. Consumers are not blameless! When they search for flights on the Internet, consumers usually have only one metric for making their choice: what does the ticket cost? They see a higher price as a loss and a lower price as a win. This win-lose view leads them to choose discount airlines (like Southwest) whenever they can. Forced to reduce their own prices, full-service airlines focus on issues that this metric does not capture. They eliminate meals, reduce legroom, and minimize the incline of the seats. They cut salaries of flight attendants, who, as a group, become increasingly discourteous. *When they are in the air*, consumers resent these acts. But *when they book their next ticket*, they forget their experiences and *again* focus solely on price. Airlines—like American—quickly learn that benefits like "more legroom in every seat" do not increase sales. Day-by-day, air travel becomes more unpleasant, because one party abuses Design Principle 1 and the other violates Design Principle 2.

To effectively implement the second Design Principle, executives must pay close attention to the metrics their companies use to evaluate both relationships with others and the people who manage them. Cost must be one of a set of key metrics, but *never* the only one. Nokia, Mr. Baril said, shifted focus from "cost reduction" to "revenue enhancement"; its staff received instructions to manage "not components, but solutions." The resultant change in metrics also covered several other functions. For example, Mr. Korhonen said, Nokia "began measuring salespeople also for inventory and measuring manufacturing people not just for costs, but also for market share and availability."

HP too tried to make this change. Mr. Scholler wanted to make procurement staff responsible not only for component costs, but also for all the other costs that must be considered to develop win-win options, such as the cost of lack of needed supplies and the cost of excess supplies. However, the company's decentralized structure made it difficult to come up with a comprehensive metric.

Recognize That It Takes Time to Overcome Distrust

Getting to win-win requires patience; we cannot easily convince people of an overnight change of heart if we have long had antagonistic relationships with them! When Mr. Baril broached the topic with a counterpart at a Global 500 company with an existing *positive* relationship with Nokia, the gentleman said, "When you say 'win-win,' do you know what it means to me? It means Nokia wins the first time and Nokia wins the second time!"

Potential partners are also skeptical about HP's initial overtures. The PRM team has to work hard, often at executive levels, to convince them—slowly. Mr. Nagali:

> For our initial pitch, we say, "Do a small pilot. If you don't see value, go back to doing what you were doing." ...We proceed very gradually and take at least a year to get our suppliers fully involved in the program.... [It] takes a year for a supplier to...use the information to make better decisions.

The slow progress can make adopting the second Design Principle particularly difficult. In most large companies, mid-level executives often stay in a position two to three years. As such, an executive may not *personally* benefit from initiating such an effort and therefore may be disinclined to take on the risk. One possible solution is senior executive sponsorship, since they typically tend to stay in their positions longer than mid-tier managers. Purely from the perspective of organizational structure and dynamics, this makes them better positioned to take a longer-term perspective.

Another possible solution is devoting significant attention to building person-to-person relationships with counterparts in partner companies. Mr. Markki said flatly, "...the value of personal relationships is underestimated." He and other Nokia executives told me several stories about how they built these relationships; given Nokia's Nordic heritage, the sauna often played a key mediating role! But even executives at a politically correct American firm believe in the critical role of personal relationships. Mr. Schneider, for example, spoke of the need to "sit...down face-to-face with people" so that "you may be able to establish a personal relationship, about hobbies, sports, family" in order to "make negotiations much less confrontational."

Nice Guys Aren't Finishing Last

Of the four Design Principles, the second is most likely to draw skepticism, because its implementation requires people and companies to change not only what they *do*, but also how they *behave*. That is indeed a very tall order.

So, people may well ask: Are Hewlett-Packard and Nokia at the tip of the arrow, or are they simply anomalies? A few years ago, it would have been impossible to tell for sure. Today, the press regularly tells stories of business leaders who would fit in at Nokia and of the downfall of those who would not. I gathered the following examples effortlessly, without mining databases, asking business associates for recommendations, or including executives I know personally. A more structured search would have uncovered many more. I deliberately picked American companies. Competition here tends to have a harder edge than in Europe, and Asia has a long history of cooperation among members of *keiretsus*[26]. All the stories describe internally directed efforts at win-win; this is a natural first step, since one cannot credibly ask outsiders to collaborate if insiders will not do so.

- After a long, ugly, public battle, Morgan Stanley dismissed its CEO, Phillip Purcell.[27] The *New York Times* article called his predecessor, Richard Fisher, "...a prototype of the modern chief executive" who encouraged discussion and disagreement and "made people feel good about themselves, and about the firm."

In contrast, executives "learned that it was pointless to argue with Mr. Purcell about anything—all it did was make him mad, and he didn't even pretend to be listening." Despite having a Board "packed with his people," the fact that Mr. Purcell failed to outmaneuver his many critics is "perhaps the most powerful evidence of how much the world has changed."

- In mid-July 2006, Pfizer replaced its CEO, Henry McKinnell.[28] Again, the *New York Times* noted, "In the past few months, analysts and people in the industry said, Pfizer's board has grown increasingly concerned about Mr. McKinnell's autocratic management style..." The article quoted a Merrill Lynch analyst as saying "Investors have been frustrated that McKinnell has run the company in somewhat of an autocratic fashion..." The new CEO, Jeffery Kindler, a relative newcomer not only to Pfizer but also to the industry, "impressed Pfizer's directors with his...leadership skills."

- Richard Parsons, who retired in late 2007, reportedly became the CEO of AOL Time Warner because he was the only person acceptable to its two warring parties, the AOL upstarts and the Time Warner patricians.[29] He lasted much longer than many analysts expected, principally by getting the two parties to work together. Along the way, he cut the company's huge debt and improved its fortunes. When Carl Icahn pressured him to dismember the company, Mr. Parsons not only preserved its structure, but also placated those allied with Mr. Icahn.[30] Mr. Parsons told *Fortune* that his predecessor, Steve Case, gave him the best advice he had ever received: "When you negotiate, leave something on the table."[31] He added: "I've used that advice a thousand times since, literally...people get hung up with their advisors...and every instance becomes a tug of war to see who can out-duel the other to get the slightest little advantage on a transaction. But people don't keep in mind that the advisors are going to move on to the next deal, while you and I are going to have to see each other again."

- In an article that proclaimed every few lines that the jury was still out, the *New York Times* observed that American Airlines is "...throwing off its famously button-down culture and endeavoring to replace management-by-edict with freewheeling collaboration."[32] CEO Gerard J. Arpey "...has traded away the bankruptcy card used by most of his competitors..." Mr. Arpey says he intends to "...make organized labor and our front-line employees our business partners" because "...the world's largest airline cannot become more efficient without such collaboration." When he took over in 2003, American was "...a command-and-control organization in danger of suffocating itself. Mr. Arpey intends to change all of that." Unlike "...his better-known mentor, Robert L. Crandall, who ran American like a drill sergeant until the late 1990s..." Mr. Arpey "...may be the better man" to "persuade...distrustful employees that management is sincere in seeking collaboration."

- *The Economist* described how Nokia rival Motorola changed after the arrival of CEO Ed Zander in January 2004:[33] In quick order, Motorola brought out three stylish phones that took market share from rivals. "One of the biggest changes at Motorola since Mr. Zander's arrival...has been in the way that different teams— from design and engineering to marketing and finance—have got together to sort out the enormous complexities involved in developing new handsets. Cooperation improved...because each group became willing to try something difficult that might help the others—without worrying too much about who would get blamed if they failed." The article continued that such change "...is hard to achieve unless the boss takes it seriously— and unless everyone...knows that the rules have changed." The cultural changes have "...filtered through to the company's hiring, where more emphasis is now being placed on people skills, rather than just technical ability. After all, when innovation involves complex interactions between many internal teams and outside partners—as it does at Motorola—the ability to communicate is prized."

The *Times* article on Morgan Stanley noted that the dethroning of Mr. Purcell was not unique. In contrast to the 1980s, tough-talking CEOs are no longer the norm. It quoted Andrea Redmond, an executive headhunter at Russell Reynolds, as saying that successful chief executives today are "inclusive, open and transparent" and "have the ability to get people to trust them" and "chief executives who lack those qualities and who rule by fear will eventually be rejected."

There is a certain irony in this. This epoch is driven by distributed computer networks that allow people to collaborate over time and across space. Yet its fate may ultimately lie in whether people can look into each other's eyes and think, "I suppose I can trust you!" In her book about the early widespread deployment of computers in the workplace, sociologist Shoshana Zuboff wondered whether we could hold people responsible for not noticing information that appeared on their computer screens (such as a momentary spike in voltage).[34] Almost twenty years later, we need to wonder whether we can trust the people *behind* the computer screens if we have never broken bread with them.

This brings us back to the discussion that opened this chapter. By its choices of two new executives for Chrysler, the private equity firm that bought Chrysler (Cerberus) unwittingly made it the proverbial canary in the coal mine for the U.S. auto industry. Co-president James Press came from Toyota, where he had a seat on the Board. He will undoubtedly try to instill into Chrysler the magic that makes Toyota a great (adaptive) company that nurtures its network. His boss, chairman Bob Nardelli, got fired by Home Depot; as CEO, he grew revenues and the numbers of stores, but he could not better its profits or share price. He also became known for authoritarian, take-no-prisoners, arrogant behavior.[35] He is supposed to cut costs and manage a turnaround; arguably, his approach to business has more in common with Mr. Lopez at GM than with the quintessential Toyota executive. Chrysler needs both types of change, but which *approach to change* actually drives managerial action will determine its real fortunes. If it is that of Mr. Press, it may actually thrive; if it is that of Mr. Nardelli—unless he has changed his spots—it will probably flounder. I hope it is Mr. Press, but I fear it will be Mr. Nardelli; the financial institutions that funded Cerberus' bid reportedly enabled his hiring.[36] In either case, during the next few years, Chrysler will be an object lesson for many.

Can Win-Win Develop Everywhere? Or, Do You Have Niceness in Your Genes?

In late 2005, I spent a day teaching about Adaptive Businesses in a custom executive program for a very large European manufacturer ("EuroCo"). The forty-odd attendees were two or three levels below its Executive Board. Early in the day, after discussing the *Wall Street Journal* article on Nokia, Ericsson, and the Philips fire, I asked them to work in small groups on a set of questions about their ability to deal with predictable surprises (see the section "What Must the Company Sense?" in Chapter 4).

Two of the five groups began their subsequent presentations by speaking of the importance of ensuring that no one would blame them if things went wrong. Later, when I spoke of the PRM program, one executive, arms crossed, announced, "I don't believe you. I won't, unless you tell me exactly how the HP software works and how much they pay. No company does anything like this." Several others murmured their agreement, and the speaker literally turned his back to me. Adaptive Business wouldn't raise its ugly head in their company! Not on their watch!

At a social event that evening, several EuroCo executives confessed to me individually—in lowered voices and never in the presence of more than one colleague—that what I had witnessed was the critical problem at EuroCo. They gave specific examples of how such attitudes were keeping EuroCo from achieving its publicly stated goals. An ongoing CEO-led effort to improve financial results by modifying strategy and improving the company's organizational effectiveness did not consider changing such attitudes a priority. These executives, despite their seniority, did not feel they could put a positive attitude toward collaboration on the agenda.

In discussing the multiperiod Prisoner's Dilemma, I wrote that research shows that a critical mass of people who believed in win-win could eventually change their win-lose community. The key term here is critical mass. In EuroCo, a dog-eat-dog belief is deeply ingrained in day-to-day behavior. Not everyone working there subscribes to such behavior, but there aren't enough such people. Mr. Baril said that win-win is "...in Nokia's genes." The same cannot be said of EuroCo.

So, You Are Not the CEO...

I wrote that I expected people to be skeptical about this Design Principle because it requires changes not just in what they do, but in how they behave. So, did you recognize yourself in this chapter? Did Mr. Baril's views on the Olympics strike a chord with you? Or do you see business inherently as a win-lose proposition? The key point to take away is, *pursue win-win for business reasons, not for altruistic reasons*. You will not be able to apply this Design Principle without accepting the validity of this assertion. So:

1. Read Robert Axelrod's (slim!) book on the Prisoner's Dilemma, *The Evolution of Cooperation* (Basic Books, 1985). If you are a believer, it will teach you to translate your beliefs into action. If you are a skeptic, it will teach you simple strategies for achieving win-win results without trying to convince you that humans are essentially good-natured.

2. Assess your company. Recognize that changes, if needed, will be hard and take time. Then ask yourself, can win-win take hold here if people try? If the answer is no, you have a decision to make about your career. If you have many productive work-life years ahead of you, remember that your company's success increasingly depends on the quality of its network relationships.

3. Here are a few things for groups of managers and professionals to do:

   - For the map of workgroups you have drawn, consider where collaboration breaks down internally and why. The first few times you do this, involve an objective third party; this will force you to confront your own failings instead of blaming others.

   - Do not try to improve cooperation in everything. Instead, focus on the two specific sense-and-respond challenges you identified in Chapter 3, "Visions from the Present." What noncooperative actions will interfere with a sensing or the assembly of a response? What specific things *that are*

> *within the control of the group dealing with these issues* can you fix?
>
> • Tackle cross-organizational collaboration only after you have cleaned house.

Endnotes

[1]"Big 3 Market Share Dips to All-Time Low," by Christine Tierney, the *Detroit News*, January 5, 2005. "Foreign Automakers Pass Detroit in Monthly Sales," by Micheline Maynard and Nick Bunkley, the *New York Times*, August 2, 2007.

[2]"Overseas Sales Results Give GM an Edge Over Toyota," by Bloomberg News, the *New York Times*, October 23, 2007. "Ford Celebrates Its Growth and Success in Russia," by Andrew Kramer, the *New York Times*, July 17, 2007.

[3]"Toyota Says It'll Be No. 1 in 2009," by the Associated Press, the *New York Times*, September 1, 2007.

[4]"In India, a $2,500 Pace Car," by Heather Timmons, the *New York Times*, October 12, 2007.

[5]"Ford Eliminating up to 30,000 Jobs and 14 Factories," by Micheline Maynard, the New York Times, January 24, 2006.

[6]"GM and Union in Deal to Cut Healthcare Benefits," by Danny Hakim et al., the *New York Times*, October 18, 2005.

[7]"Is There a Future in Ford's Future?" by Micheline Maynard, the *New York Times*, January 8, 2006.

[8]"He Still Speaks German, But with a Motown Accent," by Mark Landler, the *New York Times*, November 6, 2005.

[9]Ibid., the *New York Times*, January 8, 2006.

[10]"The Dream That Once Was Detroit," by Ben Stein, the *New York Times*, May 27, 2007.

[11]See, for example, the following: "His Family and the Family: Fords Meet at a Time of Turmoil in Autos," by Danny Hakim et al., the *New York Times*, October 19, 2005. "Ford Eliminating up to 30,000 Jobs and 14 Factories," by Micheline Maynard, the *New York Times*, January 24, 2006. "Kerkorian Aide Tells GM to Be More Like Nissan," by Micheline Maynard, the *New York Times*, January 11, 2006.

[12]"The Zoom Machine at Chrysler," by Kathleen Kerwin and David Welch, *Business Week Online*, March 21, 2005.

[13]"Why Chrysler's Thinking Big," by David Kiley, *Business Week Online*, February 13, 2006. For example: "The Dodge Magnum...is languishing on dealer lots despite positive reviews in the auto press. And the Dodge Charger is not the homerun that the Chrysler 300 sedan has been.... But here's the oil slick around the corner: Chrysler's unsold inventories and incentives already rank highest among its competitors'. 2007 could end up a different story if Chrysler's fashion sense is not what it needs it to be."

[14]"Running on Empty," from the Editorial Desk at the *New York Times*, October 5, 2005.

[15]"José Ignacio López de Arriortúa," by Professors Michael H. Moffett and William E. Youngdahl, © 1998 Thunderbird, the American Graduate School of International Management.

[16]This is true of knowledge that has not been reduced to formulae, software, detailed drawings, and other, similar forms, not for knowledge that has been formulated for transfer to something else (such as patents). This is why reverse-engineering efforts often result in imperfect copies, but detailed patents do not.

[17]"Cures for Some Ailing Cars," by Scott Sturgis, the *New York Times*, May 20, 2007.

[18]"Hardware-in-the-Loop: Assuring Performance & Quality by Combining the Real & the Virtual," by Gary Vasilash, *Automotive Design & Production*, http://www.autofieldguide.com.

[19]"Behind Toyota's Software Recall," by Nicole Lewis, http://www.DSO.com, December 21, 2005.

[20]Fujimoto coauthored (with former Harvard Business School Dean Kim Clark) *Product Development Performance*, Harvard Business School Press, 1991. Unmatched in depth and breadth of research since then, it reported on the work of companies that sold 90% of the world output of automobiles in the late 1980s.

[21]Since Delphi and Visteon are former divisions of GM and Ford, respectively, treating them as separate companies would raise the degree of outsourced manufacturing.

[22]In order to focus on issues important to Adaptive Behavior, this description simplifies many technical issues whose resolution have won the PRM program numerous awards. These are described in many articles that appear in professional journals; two are listed next.

[23]Two of many articles that describe PRM in detail are "Hewlett-Packard wins for the 2nd time," by James Carbone, *Purchasing Magazine Online*, September 2, 2004, and "Procurement Risk Management (PRM) at Hewlett-Packard Company," by Venu Nagali et al., an HP manuscript created for the Council of Supply Chain Management Professionals.

[24]"Emphasize ADC and Software," *Frontline Solutions*, October 1, 2004.

[25]*The Evolution of Cooperation*, by Robert M. Axelrod, New York: Basic Books, 1984.

[26]A keiretsu is a set of companies with interlocking business relationships and shareholdings. It is a type of business group. (http://en.wikipedia.org/wiki/Keiretsu)

[27]"In Business, Tough Guys Finish Last," by Joseph Nocera, the *New York Times*, June 18, 2005.

[28]"A Long Shot Becomes Pfizer's Latest Chief Executive," by Alex Berenson, the *New York Times*, June 29, 2006.

[29]"Dick Parsons Knows What You Think," by David Carr, the *New York Times*, June 13, 2005.

[30]"Time Warner and Icahn Reach a Settlement," by Richard Siklos and Andrew Sorkin, the *New York Times*, February 18, 2006.

[31]"The Best Advice I Ever Got," by interviewers and Julia Boorstin, *Fortune*, March 21, 2005.

[32]"Anger Management at American Air," by Jeff Bailey, the *New York Times*, July 23, 2006.

[33]"The Cutting Edge," *The Economist*, October 7, 2006.

[34]*In the Age of the Smart Machine*, by Shoshana Zuboff, New York: Basic Books, 1998.

[35]"Once Tainted, Nardelli Now Has Chrysler's Keys," by Micheline Maynard, the *New York Times*, August 7, 2007.

[36]"Even Chrysler Officials Were Surprised at New Owner's Leadership Choice," by Micheline Maynard, the *New York Times*, August 10, 2007.

6

Ensure That Work Teaches

An MBA elective called "Projects in Operations Management" typically attracts only a small group of engineers interested in manufacturing and the supply chain. In 1993, a diverse group of INSEAD business school students defied this norm after I promised to use manufacturing simply as a lens to focus on the general manager's challenge, "How do we make money?" We would visit factories in very different industries and bring back to the classroom issues ranging from sales management to technology creation. Ultimately, we visited five blue-chip global businesses:

- **WhiteGoodsCo:** This plant produced all the top-loading washers that WhiteGoodsCo made in Europe. Its challenges were comparable to those of other, similar plants worldwide: Match production levels and variety to market needs and reduce costs each year.

- **MaterialsCo:** This company "grew" crystals—used in medical devices and high-tech equipment—from sand. The selling price of a single perfect crystal could exceed the factory's total payroll costs. However, once the six-month-long production process commenced, the staff could do very little to detect or correct any problem.

- **Bekaert (steel wire):** The industry's basic technology has not changed in over a century. A half-inch diameter "rod" is progressively pulled through dies until it is reduced to a thread. Dozens of threads are then wound together to create a cable. While also reducing costs, the factory had to achieve quality levels unimaginable in comparison to historical performance.

- **FiberCo (fiber optoelectronics):** In this emerging technology, product generations were becoming obsolete every six months, while processes were changing sharply annually. At the factory, located near FiberCo's R&D center, people in white lab coats worked at tables equipped with powerful computers and high-tech microscopes. The company regularly transferred staff between R&D and manufacturing.

- **ConsumerCo (consumer packaged goods/chemicals):** This state-of-the-art factory produced most of France's consumption of ConsumerCo's personal health products. ConsumerCo had reengineered the manufacturing process to enable the production of batches that ranged from a few kilograms to thousands. Quick connect linkages and modular, reconfigurable assembly lines enabled a version of Lean Enterprise unlike that in any other chemical facility.

Each company had its own set of managerial challenges, derived in large part from the specific characteristics of its industry. For example, WhiteGoodsCo, ConsumerCo, and Bekaert aggressively managed costs, but FiberCo and MaterialsCo did not. However, copies of student reports and my own notes and recollections reminded me of the following:

- WhiteGoodsCo focused on continuous improvement, and its workers were adept at identifying and resolving local problems. However, it seemed unable to routinely share key information (that could improve its overall performance) across functional areas.

- MaterialsCo recognized that its processes, mostly black art, could be improved only if it collaborated with suppliers, customers, employees, and industry experts to create the needed knowledge. Yet, it mistrusted outsiders; it had multiple equipment suppliers so that none would know its plant design. This unresolved dilemma allowed competitive threats to increase.

- FiberCo dealt with technological change by tying manufacturing closely to R&D, but it could not simultaneously manage the transfer of short-term market needs from sales to the plant and medium-term market needs from sales to R&D. These difficulties kept it from producing enough output to meet demand and allowed a competing technology to gain a foothold.

- ConsumerCo created up to one hundred different products a day in production runs that varied greatly in size. This required sophisticated coordination across sales, manufacturing, engineering, and suppliers because the laws of chemistry that governed the operation of the production vats did not match the rhythm of market needs.

In these companies (and at Bekaert), one competence—*the ability to learn from the experience of working across functional and/or organizational boundaries*—seemed critical to success. What they had to learn differed, but the fact that they had to did not. However, except for Bekaert, *they either seemed oblivious to this need or could not develop the capability to do so.* They created knowledge for day-to-day work almost purely by chance. They had no people, organizational structures, policies, processes, or culture to make learning happen routinely.

Eighteen years later, though many managers know Peter Senge's name and some have helped make *The Fifth Discipline* a publishing phenomenon, most companies still do not consider the ability to learn a key executive skill, let alone an essential corporate capability. Executives are often skeptical about this assertion, so I ask, "How often are your job postings a series of must-haves and must-knows? How often is 'Must be willing to learn and change' a *top* criterion for filling critical positions, since things that are important today probably won't be tomorrow, and issues that are ignored today may be critical tomorrow?" Defensiveness usually replaces the skepticism.

Researchers call the capability I am describing "organizational learning" (see the following sidebar titled "A Primer on Organizational Learning"). I will define it as follows: *A company pursues organizational learning if it routinely and ethically enables its people to improve their knowledge of its environment and ensures that the private*

knowledge of an individual becomes the public knowledge of many.[1]
Five elements of this definition merit elucidation:

- **Routinely:** A company that suddenly "gets religion," perhaps in a moment of crisis, is not pursuing organizational learning. When I taught manufacturing, I used to say, *Every act of production should be an act of learning.* This goal should be extended to all functions.

- **Ethically:** You might have heard the adage "You can fool some of the people all of the time, and all of the people some of the time, but you cannot fool all of the people all of the time." If a company behaves unethically—for example, by usurping someone's knowledge and then replacing him or her with someone cheaper—people will resist sharing their private knowledge. Such a company may learn occasionally, but it certainly will not be able to learn continually.

- **Enables:** A company that simply encourages its people to learn, but does nothing to help them do so, is not pursuing organizational learning. It simply—and selfishly—hopes to benefit at the expense of its employees. In such an environment, learning is likely to be sporadic.

- **Environment:** This term refers to both the external environment such as customers, competitors, and economic trends, and the internal environment, which includes the work performed and the conditions that accompany its performance.

- **Private knowledge/public knowledge:** If an individual learns something valuable, he or she may benefit from it. For the organization to benefit, the individual typically must share that knowledge with others. Unless *private* knowledge is made public (within reasonable bounds of confidentiality), it is not *organizational*.

Distributed computer networks and their associated trends have increased the importance of managing learning. Today WhiteGoodsCo would have to deal with electronic components, an explosion of product models, and fractured supply-and-demand networks. It would face a greater need to share knowledge cross-functionally and cross-organizationally. If it had a sense-and-respond capability, it would have to learn to isolate "real" signals from the "noise" of the normal ebb and flow of interactions with many partners. It would also need to assess the implications of changes in industry boundaries (and shifts in customer needs and new technologies) so that it could appropriately modify its existing sense-and-respond capabilities and partnerships.

More generally, unless a company learns by collecting, analyzing, and intelligently sharing knowledge, it can neither effectively design its network nor act decisively through it. If Nokia had not been able to learn from its 1995 experience, it might have shared Ericsson's fate in 2000. If it had not been able to interpret the signs emerging from Philips in March 2000, having a sense-and-respond capability and win-win partnerships would not have helped.

Companies that aspire to be adaptive must adopt the third Design Principle: ***value and nurture organizational learning.*** *This Principle is the energizing spark that drives all aspects of adaptive behavior.* When I first presented the Adaptive Business framework to Pertti Korhonen, he sat silently, staring at it. After a minute had passed, anxious about his silence, I tried to explain. He impatiently waved a hand and demanded silence. I sank back into my chair. Some time later, he looked up, stabbed the diagram with a finger, and said,

> Learning—in the middle—is essential to translate what you get out of sense-and-respond to plan-and execute. In other words, you sense and respond. The next time you build a plan, you try to include in it what you learned when you sensed and responded.

To *consciously* implement this Design Principle, executives must understand the range of learning styles that can be observed in business settings. Not every style is effective, and knowing the range can facilitate behavioral change. Moreover, in order to move from encouraging learning to enabling it, executives must also know how organizational infrastructure supports or impedes learning.

A Primer on Organizational Learning

The field of organizational learning has not contributed as much to management practice as it could have. I attribute at least part of this failure to an unnecessary battle over semantics. For years, researchers have debated the differences between *learning* and *knowledge* and *learning organizations* and *organizational learning*. Even today, published articles try to clarify the distinctions while they add *knowledge management*, an IT-driven concept, to the mix. (For example, "Can the practice of *knowledge management* enable *organizational learning* in a firm? Is such a firm a *learning organization*?") In this chapter, I have avoided such semantic debates and relied on the "business English" meanings of terms like knowledge and learning. Moreover, since people typically learn to solve business problems by solving similar problems, I have not distinguished learning from problem solving.

The ideas I have discussed here are based on my own research, but I also draw on the works of several scholars, including those listed here.[2] My summaries are simply meant to introduce basic ideas, not to foster academic debate, so they are not as rigorous as some may desire.

Chris Argyris and Donald A. Schon (*Organizational Learning: A Theory of Action Perspective*) coined the terms Single Loop and Double Loop learning. Improving an existing sense-and-respond system based on experience is an example of the former; identifying the need for and creating a sense-and-respond system is an example of the latter. Companies are far better at Single Loop than Double Loop learning and must improve their ability to do the latter.

Peter M. Senge (*The Fifth Discipline: The Art & Practice of the Learning Organization*) wants managers to acquire five "competencies": Personal Mastery (continually aspire to improve), Mental Models (examine—and be open to changing—the assumptions and generalizations that drive perceptions of reality), Shared Vision (develop a common picture of what people want to create), Team Learning, and Systems Thinking (most cause-and-effect relationships are simplistic; they focus on issues that are "close" in time and space and ignore complexities that hide the true links). The last competency should shape the others.

Richard R. Nelson and Sidney G. Winter (*An Evolutionary Theory of Economic Change*) argue that just as individuals develop skills, organizations develop routines, or patterns of behavior. Routines belong to organizations, not individuals, and therefore may survive even if an individual is no longer in the organization. Over time, successful organizations choose from among possibly competing routines and adopt/apply the ones that best serve their competitive purposes.

Jean Lave and Etienne Wenger (*Situated Learning: Legitimate Peripheral Participation*) created the idea of "communities of practice." These are groups of people who share a common interest. By developing and improving a *shared* language and resources, a community of practice creates (and improves) its own understanding of its interests. Activity and knowledge are comingled; people who congregate for a brown-bag lecture aren't a community.

Graham T. Allison (*Essence of Decision: Explaining the Cuban Missile Crisis*) shows that, contrary to conventional assumptions (Rational Actor paradigm) in vast areas of human knowledge (for example, economics), people do not objectively assess their options and pursue organizational goals. Instead, they follow well-established routines in their workgroups (Organizational Behavior paradigm) that change very slowly, unless a major crisis occurs. Moreover, people are influenced by their personal and local work unit's goals (Government Political paradigms). These goals lead to negotiation with peers about the correctness of decisions.

How People Learn to Solve Business Problems

How do people learn to solve business problems? The knee-jerk answer, based on long exposure to the idea of the "learning curve," is "by accumulating experience."[3] This response is not only a terrible example of circular logic, but it also begs the question of whether experience can accumulate more effectively in some environments than in others.

Managers can create great learning environments! As the Adaptive Business epoch was emerging, Ramchandran Jaikumar was helping Bekaert embark on an ambitious effort to use knowledge for competitive advantage. Its then-CEO, Karel Vinck, allowed me to study how managers, engineers, scientists, and line workers learned to solve complex, messy problems and how infrastructural decisions either helped or hindered them.[4] He gave me complete access to the staff, facilities, and documents in its Research, Development, and Manufacturing groups. After I became an INSEAD faculty member, Bekaert's next CEO, Rafael Decaluwé, allowed a three-person team that I then led to extend the work.[5, 6] Over the course of a decade, my colleagues and I studied in great detail seventy two projects that Bekaert's staff had executed over several years.

People usually learn to solve complex business problems by first observing more experienced colleagues tackle similar problems. They then develop their own instincts by trial and error, often under the tutelage of such a colleague. For example, at a food company I knew well, new bakers were trained by master bakers. Initially, the latter demonstrated each step. They taught the novices how to tease balls of dough into membranes and assess the level of force necessary to tear these. They also taught them how to touch the product just before the final production step to see if it had a "nice skin." The novices then made many batches of the product under the masters' watchful eyes.

The masters cajoled and scolded and encouraged the apprentices and finally pronounced them trained. Acquiring the full competence to solve all the problems that could arise often took a year of daily work. In a very similar manner, newly hired loan officers in many a commercial bank learn how to structure loans by observing their more experienced colleagues do so. They must learn that when the bank provides mezzanine financing, it tolerates a higher level of debt and a thinner cushion in projected cash flows than when it provides "Tier 1" financing. The exact levels of acceptability may differ from industry to industry, by timing in the business cycle, and by a host of other explicit and implicit factors.

I call such learning *experiential* to recognize the role of *repeated contact* with a diverse set of work-related situations. Experiential learning teaches people two things. First, they learn to *recognize events that require action*. For example, the baker must learn when the membrane is "weak," and the new banker must learn when a client's risk profile has changed substantially. Second, experiential learning teaches people *how to react* to these events. What should the baker do if the membrane keeps tearing or the skin feels "wet?" What should the banker do if the cash-flow levels seem acceptable but the debt levels seem somewhat high?

The less common way that people learn to solve business problems is by first understanding *why* different elements of their work interact in particular ways. I call such learning *conceptual* to recognize the critical role of theory.[7] For example, a baker might learn about the physical and chemical changes that occur in wheat gluten during the mixing of dough and the consequent changes in the dough's "elastic modulus." Changes that produce certain levels of elastic modulus make the membrane strong. The banker could learn "stress tests" to conduct, which would allow her to evaluate the true "quality of earning," given her bank's expectations of the macroeconomic environment in which its potential client would operate. Both the baker and the banker could learn everything he or she needed by reading, modeling, solving problems, or working with well-designed simulation models. An "expert" could help elucidate a theory for the benefit of a novice but would not be central to the learning process.

No one uses one or the other learning mode exclusively. Indeed, we combine different levels of experiential and conceptual learning when we search for solutions to business challenges. The FIRE model shown in Table 6-1 illustrates that *the choices we make have a profound impact on our effectiveness.*

TABLE 6-1   Modes of Knowledge/Learning: the FIRE Model

		Experiential Knowledge/Learning	
		Low	**High**
Conceptual Knowledge/Learning	**Low**	Firefight	Routinize
	High	Intellectualize	Empiricalize

- An *ineffective* mode—from the perspective of achieving results, resources needed, and the elapsed time—is to *firefight*. People rely on this mode—which combines low levels of experiential and conceptual knowledge—when they throw possible solutions at a problem and hope that something sticks. If the problem is particularly obdurate, they sometimes go into crisis mode and *simultaneously* attempt many possible solutions. Typically, they have no idea why the problem has arisen or why a particular option might work. The data from Bekaert shows that over time, firefighting produces no discernable benefits.

- An even *worse* choice of modes is to ***intellectualize*** the effort by relying heavily on conceptual knowledge. Most business-related models (for example, macroeconomic theory or marketing segments) are *imperfect* representations of the real world. Consequently, intellectualizing is susceptible to disruptions from subtle but critical features of the real world that are not included in the models.[8] Data shows that this mode of problem solving actually worsens performance over time.

- The most popular approach to business problem solving is to **routinize** it by applying formal tools like Six Sigma to experiential knowledge. This mode is *somewhat effective*. The tools help sort fact from fiction but cannot always uncover deeper facts. Data shows that routinizing does have immediate impact, but rarely do the benefits last over the medium or long term.

- The *most effective* mode for solving problems is to **empiricalize** the effort. This mode of problem solving combines a high level of conceptual knowledge with an equally high level of experiential knowledge. Stated another way, human intuition is routinely checked against known models of the world; conversely, models are subjected to tests of reasonableness before action is taken. The research at Bekaert showed that this mode of problem solving produces the greatest long-term benefits.

To apply the empiricalized mode, people must ask, What are we trying to prove or understand? How will we change the operating conditions? How will we *unambiguously* observe and measure the results? What factors could confound our efforts? How will we control these? *Who will document what we learn and broadcast it to all who might benefit?*

The empiricalized approach has enabled Toyota (which is an Adaptive Business) to sustain its advantage over its rivals even though they have emulated its Lean methodology. Steven Spear, who described how learning powered Toyota, asserted that without a similar commitment, no one could claim to be Lean.[9] Spear listed four "rules," including "Any improvement must be made in accordance with the scientific method, under the guidance of a teacher..." He also listed four "lessons" that Toyota managers learn, including "Proposed changes should always be structured as experiments" and "Workers and managers must experiment as frequently as possible." Staff learn to carefully observe their environment, precisely predict benefits they expect from proposed changes, and assess whether the implemented changes actually produce the *predicted* result. Changes whose benefits *exceed* predictions are as unacceptable as changes whose benefits fall short; *any* mismatch implies a lack of understanding of all relevant issues.

Empiricalized learning is critical for Adaptive Businesses. As the complexity of their network rises, business models can lose applicability across organizational, geographic, and temporal locales. Simultaneously, complexity also limits the power of old experiences to explain issues spanning organizations, geography, and time. Empiricalized learning enables people to quickly develop valid, *shared* understanding of their world, because combining both types of knowledge may enable each to compensate for the weaknesses of the other.

Creating a Learning Organization

By encouraging empiricalized knowledge/learning, executives can make private knowledge public. To *enable* its *routine* use, they have to think about the impact of three key elements of their companies—processes, organizational structure, and the culture.[10]

Processes

The noun "process" refers to a series of actions, changes, operations, or functions that produce a result or create or modify a product or service.[11] The use of this term exploded after Michael Hammer and James Champy wrote *Reengineering the Corporation*.[12] They took an idea that was hitherto prized only by people in manufacturing/operations and software design and showed general managers how to apply it throughout the company. One could start with the end product or service being delivered and identify all the actions, changes, operations, or functions, as well as the decisions and uncertainties, that went into creating it. One could then reengineer these so that they worked together effectively and efficiently. This would not only improve quality, but also would reduce costs by eliminating waste.

Without a doubt, processes are here to stay, and the world is better off for them. Indeed, many of the ideas in this book—such as building sense-and-respond capabilities—will require the creation or revision of processes.

Nevertheless, processes are double-edged swords for organizational learning. On the one hand, they enable managers to ensure that new ideas are routinely used. John Bowman is a member of an internal consulting group that advises HP's senior management. This group creates empiricalized knowledge that often incorporates mathematical models. He argues,

> Institutionalizing knowledge to a large extent means designing a business process that reflects that knowledge and getting it adopted.

In other words, the most effective way to convert private knowledge into public knowledge is to embed the knowledge into a business process. When I asked him if the knowledge his group created could be transferred to other companies, Mr. Bowman noted that his group often trades knowledge with a similar group at Proctor & Gamble. For other companies, he said:

> A fair number of our [knowledge embedded] tools...can be applied outside HP.... However, without business processes, other companies may not be able to use these effectively...

On the other hand, processes are natural outcomes of the plan-and-execute paradigm. When a company reengineers its processes, it takes a hard look at the external and internal environments and specifies what must be done (plan). Thereafter, people work in accordance with the process that is defined (execute), usually unquestioningly. This fact surfaces a problem that is best described by a story that a renowned historian, MIT professor Elting E. Morison, told in 1950:[13]

> In the early days of the last war, when armaments of all kinds were in short supply, the British, I am told, made use of a venerable field piece that had come down to them from previous generations. The honorable past of this light artillery

stretched back, in fact, to the Boer War. In the days of uncertainty after the fall of France, these guns, hitched to trucks, served as useful mobile units in the coast defense. But it was felt that the rapidity of fire could be increased. A time-motion expert was, therefore, called in to suggest ways to simplify the firing procedures. He watched one of the gun crews of five men at practice in the field for some time. Puzzled by certain aspects of the procedures, he took some slow-motion pictures of the soldiers performing the loading, aiming, and firing routines. When he ran these pictures over once or twice, he noticed something that appeared odd to him. A moment before the firing, two members of the gun crew ceased all activity and came to attention for a three-second interval extending throughout the discharge of the gun. He summoned an old colonel of artillery, showed him the pictures, and pointed out this strange behavior. What, he asked the colonel, did it mean? The colonel, too, was puzzled. He asked to see the pictures again. "Ah," he said when the performance was over, "I have it. They are holding the horses."

The problem then, is this: Once processes are defined, companies generally adhere to them as if they are cavalry horses, to be held even when they are not present—and the British Army of sixty seven years ago isn't the only culprit. An experienced manager at a top global bank recently noted with frustration that at the start of virtually *every* work-week, she receives an e-mail from the Six Sigma Black Belt in her group. The e-mail includes a process map of some trivial aspect of the work her group does. Yet she devotes valuable time to respond—in accordance with the bank's Six Sigma policy—to this unnecessary work. This particular cavalry horse was put into place by an executive officer; no one dares to point out its worthlessness.

Moreover, even if improvements are made *within* the bounds of a process, the company may not be able to make more improvements *to* the process. A former colleague at INSEAD, Professor James Teboul, used to rail at the adoption of the ISO 9000 process certifications by European companies. He would draw a stick figure pushing a ball up a hill and add a "right triangular backstop" labeled "ISO 9000" behind the stick figure.[14] An expert on quality, he would passionately argue that ISO 9000 was good only for preventing companies from slipping back on quality; it would not help them push the ball up the hill. Teboul felt that the certifications would make it harder for them to change and improve. Yet the companies persisted in eagerly hanging this millstone from their necks.

This generic problem is particularly important for Adaptive Businesses to track, because it may prevent the modification of an outdated sense-and-respond process. Indeed, Nokia believes that although processes are necessary, they can be detrimental to learning, experimenting, and improvement. Jean-Francois Baril drew an analogy:

> I love to cook. I don't follow a recipe. Just following a recipe is boring. You *never* create great dishes. Doesn't mean you don't have recipes, though. Similarly, we have a lot of processes. We try to extend the processes. If we only follow the processes, we will never be exceptional. I begin with the process, and then I try to be creative.

Executives must ask regularly: *Does the (insert name) process help us get better over time?* If it does not, unless it deals with regulatory or safety issues, it will do more damage in the long term. To determine whether it does, they must ask: *How does this process help us identify and resolve new and/or emerging problems? Have we ensured that thoughtful staff will be able to experimentally modify the process itself to see if it can be improved?* Asking these questions routinely—and acting on the answers—can be more powerful than once-in-a-blue-moon business-process reengineering efforts.[15] The approach is not easy, for it raises several policy questions: What threshold of expected benefits must be crossed before a process change is seriously considered? How much experimentation with process changes—regardless of benefits—is acceptable over a given period of time? Who will have the right to authorize such an experimentation? What mechanism will ensure that changes made to improve one process locally does not have adverse effects on other processes?

Organizational Structure

The second of the three elements that affects a company's ability to learn is its organizational structure.[16] Whereas processes *if embedded with knowledge* (as Mr. Bowman suggested) enable *passive* use of knowledge, organizational structure can drive *active* use by pointing out what knowledge exists and how learning could be managed.

One key role that structure can play is being the *gatekeeper* and evaluating knowledge to assess whether it is valuable enough to retain. In this role, the gatekeeper is often a specific group of people formed for the purpose; the group may be temporary or permanent. HP uses a temporary structure at the conclusion of a project. Vice President Eric Schneider, leader of its high-volume server business:

> At the conclusion of any type of project—for example, at the end of a product launch, where we may have forecast certain revenues, launch dates, and costs—we have a *post mortem* effort. What were our actual revenues and profits? For another example, if a factory is shut down for a few days, we would put together a [cross-functional] team to assess what went wrong and what we need to change. *The idea is not to point fingers, but to learn how to do better.*

I believe that an equally important benefit (which HP executives did not articulate) is that the *post mortem* team collectively keeps an individual's potentially false beliefs about cause and effect from gaining credence in the organizational memory. Doing so is critically important because research shows that even honest, well-meaning people tend to attribute good outcomes to actions they initiated and bad outcomes to luck and the actions of others. A well structured, routinely done *post mortem* can substantially reduce the possibility of false learning.

HP relies on semipermanent organizational structures—standing cross-functional teams—for ongoing efforts like the PRM. Mr. Schneider's group, for example, has its own *post mortem* facilitator, who has a dotted-line relationship with Venu Nagali. It also uses cross-functional "core teams" (a "community of practice," as described in the section "Create Self-Contained Learning Organizations" later in this chapter) to conduct *post mortems* on specific standing topics like memory chips. This core team has as its members people from supply chain, procurement, marketing, and product development and people with industry-specific knowledge. The marketer can address challenges of product promotions, the product developer can address life cycle issues, and an industry expert may have strong links to external partners.

The second role that organizational structure plays is being a *repository of critical knowledge and an active facilitator of its use.* The internal consulting team that Mr. Bowman belongs to fulfills this particular role. Mr. Bowman:

> ...because of our role, we see the same suggestions appear year after year, particularly when a new manager comes in. We've been asked to work on the same problem three times, and we say, "Why don't you ask Joe first?" ...On the flip side, when you have a *de facto* centralized knowledge repository, it is easier to manage organizational learning. But it never gets easy. We've been struggling with it for a number of years.

The head of the consulting team to which Mr. Bowman belongs also chairs a standing committee of senior executives that makes connections between business groups that can help each other. One group may possess some knowledge needed by another or may have solved some problem currently afflicting another. Mr. Bowman:

> Within each group, a great deal of...work is done. The results of these efforts are shared through the Council.... The point is that they really can learn from each other, *not* that the [solution] will pretty much be the same all the time.

Organizational structure also plays a key role at Nokia, but it takes a very different form. Here too, project teams and standing workgroups engage in regular—weekly—"lessons learned" debriefings, but there the similarity ends. Mr. Baril drew parallels to the management of quality:

Being good at learning is analogous to being good at quality. The best-quality companies you see have very few people in their central quality department. Quality spirit and processes are fully embedded in all organizations.

Consistent with this view, Nokia decentralizes and distributes learning and managing knowledge across all managers. There are no specialized, central groups to serve as clearinghouses of information. Nokia fears that such groups could signal that only a handful of people bear the responsibility for learning.

Culture

The last of the elements that affect an organization's ability to learn is its culture. Here, three traits are critically important. The easiest of these to prescribe is *being open to outside influences*. Mr. Baril:

> We try to develop curiosity to go outside. We try to be open with our model. We talk to different suppliers and see what *we* need to adopt from *them*.

This perspective is a simple reversal of Nokia's views on sharing of information that underpins its win-win policy. Management gurus have long recommended its adoption by companies, but few do so well. This failure can be attributed to the intertwining of the refusal to accept ideas originated by outsiders (the so-called "not invented here [NIH] syndrome") with the fact that most knowledge acquired in this fashion is experiential. Experiential knowledge allows NIH syndrome to grow strong roots, because it makes it easy for people to deny the usefulness of a new idea that does not work immediately.

A second critical trait is *a willingness to take risks*. To encourage their people to constantly learn, companies must encourage them to try things that they have not done before. All such efforts involve risk, so Mr. Baril said, "We authorize people to take risks." Mr. Korhonen explained how this authorization is actually transformed into action:

We set challenging targets. To reach the targets, it is not enough to continue to do the same that you were doing last year. You have to rebuild the business to reach the targets. The business is so complex that unless you are learning, developing all the time, you don't get ahead.

In other words, challenging goals, backed by management support, move conversation and thinking inexorably from "It's too risky" to "We need to figure it out." In so doing, they set people on the path of learning.

The final critical cultural trait is *a willingness to learn from mistakes*. Mr. Schneider noted that groups participating in *post mortem* analyses understand that "It is OK to be hard at results, but not OK to be mad at the people." Indeed, without this trait, *post mortem* analyses would quickly turn into EuroCo's dysfunctional behavior: blame others while shielding yourself.

Ironically, everyday "good management practices" keep companies from adopting this last trait. One example is a single-minded desire for "accountability." Always holding people responsible for the consequences of their actions induces them to play it safe. Prudence becomes the watchword; innovation, taking bold steps, and the learning necessary to do both regularly are avoided. Molehills become mountains by the time juniors bring their errors to the attention of their superiors. Mr. Korhonen made this case as he explained how CEO Jorma Ollila came to press Nokia's case directly with Philips' CEO after the fire:

> Where people are punished for mistakes, do you tell your manager you have a problem? Probably not. You try to act to solve the problem yourself. Often you can solve it. But if you cannot, it escalates and becomes bigger and bigger, and by the time the CEO knows about it, the problem has become very big. [When the fire occurred, we] had an escalation route, and we could go to the CEO. He saw himself as the chief buyer. It wasn't the first time we needed his help with a supplier. We had developed this way of operating. And when the call came

to him, he knew it was serious. In another culture, he would have said, "This is not my problem. You get paid to solve it." But he said, "What can I do to help?"

Another example is the ABC performance evaluation model popularized by GE. The assumption behind this model is that in most companies, management fails to spend enough time with their "A players" because they focus too much on problems created by the "C players." The advocated solution? *Every year*, fire the "C players" and "upgrade" the talent pool. Mr. Korhonen disdainfully said that to foster a culture of learning, "there are some things we don't do." The ABC system is anathema because "What does that do for learning? They don't want to share—because they won't be better than their colleagues."

The inability to let go of these two "good management practices" will make this trait—*a willingness to learn from mistakes*—hard for many companies to accept. Nokia executives were not the first to reject these practices. Edward Deming, who—together with Joseph Juran—was the motivating force behind the modern quality movement, railed against such evaluation systems throughout his life. He used the laws of statistics to teach executives that the logic embodied in these was grossly flawed. In recent years, several companies have dropped the ABC system due to fears of class-action lawsuits. The open question is whether the alternatives they adopt will forsake strict accountability.

So how does management retain control at Nokia? First, it is very clear about mistakes that will *not* be tolerated. Mr. Baril said that Nokia staff could err "without fear" as long as their actions are "within the frame of our values." Second, to ensure that problems do not spiral out of control, it insists on openness and sharing. I asked Mr. Korhonen what long-term impact the fire had had on Nokia. The man who had said that it was a bigger deal outside the company than inside unhesitatingly referred to the publicity and said it reinforced for Nokia staff "how important it was to be honest and transparent in our culture."

Implementing the Third Design Principle

While each of the three elements—process, organization, and culture—have a unique role to play, they *collectively* constitute the engine for organizational learning, as shown in Figure 6-1. *Either by evolution or by design, they mutually reinforce each other's effect on a company's learning abilities.*

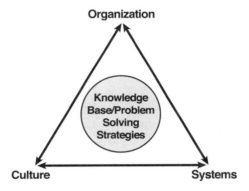

Figure 6-1 A model of organizational learning

For example, recall that the learning engines in place at HP and Nokia differ significantly on one of the dimensions—organizational structure. HP relies on a formally structured, high-powered, internal group that is staffed mostly by Ph.D.s to be the gatekeeper and storehouse of critical knowledge. Nokia relies on its managerial hierarchy to manage knowledge creation. Is either company better off than the other? The answer is a resounding no.

The three elements collectively create the learning strategy that each company uses. Nokia works almost exclusively within a relatively narrow band of products. It is relatively centralized, its processes are largely uniform and consistent across the world, and its culture is remarkably strong and uniform. Its *decentralized management of learning* facilitates numerous instances of *local* experimentation. The best ideas that result can then be adopted centrally. In contrast, HP is a highly decentralized company in which different business units that serve different markets have different policies, processes, and, to some extent, culture.[17] In this *diverse* environment, a *centralized group* can facilitate the effective creation and sharing of knowledge. If Nokia adopted HP's structure, there would no longer be any mechanism to encourage people to think and solve problems they faced locally. If HP adopted Nokia's structure, each business unit would pretty much operate on its own, neither learning from others nor sharing its knowledge.

Mutual reinforcement also implies that changing one of the elements of the learning engine will not meaningfully improve capabilities; without concomitant changes in the others, the initial change will get suppressed. This is why even well-meaning, well-managed companies have great difficulty becoming learning organizations. A nifty approach to learning that is delivering great value in one organization may be perfectly emulated by others and still not generate value because critical supporting elements are missing. Such failures were common in the 1980s when Western companies scrambled to adopt Quality Circles (an organizational structure) and the Seven Statistical Tools (a problem-solving process). But they did not adopt the cultural underpinnings that made these elements key attributes of successful Japanese companies.

These two propositions imply that the best way to become a learning organization is to build the right culture, organization, and processes from the start. For established firms, they may seem to suggest that companies that are good at knowledge creation will continue to get better at it, while others will find it impossible to improve. However, this logic is not absolute. With care and effort, companies can become learning organizations by applying the propositions instead of fighting them. The sidebar titled "Creating a Learning Organization: The Model Lines of Bekaert" describes how one company—and, in particular, a mid-level manager—blazed its own path. More generally, companies can adopt three strategies, as described next.

Creating a Learning Organization: The Model Lines of Bekaert

In the late 1980s, a remarkable effort to create usable, transferable knowledge began at the multinational company Bekaert. Influenced by Jai, then Bekaert's CEO, Karel Vinck personally sponsored the effort, which—because of the company's business needs—focused on technology and manufacturing. Since the factory environment was much too complex for such a risky experiment, Bekaert set up a self-contained learning organization, which it called Model Line-Aalter (ML-A) at its Aalter (Belgium) plant.

Paul Dambre, an experienced R&D engineer, left his laboratories to lead the ML-A. His organization, a tiny team of young and experienced staff, worked with the foremen and technical specialists running various production steps. The ML-A focused on one key product and created a process to link every resource needed to make it. The process enabled the ML-A to collect data on virtually everything that could possibly affect the product. Culturally, Mr. Dambre focused his team on one goal: *create usable knowledge daily during full-scale production.*

Mr. Dambre's background initially led him to believe that intellectualized problem solving would help Bekaert. His team did use formal chemical models that R&D created to solve a few complex, critical problems. However, he soon learned that unmodified models worked better on test benches than in the plant. As the ML-A adopted empiricalized knowledge, its problem-solving effectiveness increased, and its findings became transferable to other plants.

Buoyed by this success, Bekaert asked Mr. Dambre to start up other MLs focused on different products in other plants. Each ML created and transferred knowledge across the system. Not all were effective, but undeniably, the transfer of knowledge ensured that each new ML started at a higher level of performance than the ones that had preceded it.

But what of the world outside the MLs? R&D staff swore by their intellectualized knowledge and manufacturing staff, by their routinized knowledge. Mr. Dambre did not challenge either directly, but at an open meeting that he regularly held to discuss the ML-A's work, I saw him use the power of his position shrewdly. When a relatively senior manager expressed an opinion about an issue, Mr. Dambre asked, "You've got data?" The manager replied that he was drawing on his experience. Mr. Dambre replied, "Please sit down. You cannot talk in my meeting if you don't have data." When another engineer brought up a comparatively trivial issue and referred to his data, Mr. Dambre explored it at great length. In a matter of months, the use of empiricalized knowledge became common. Mr. Dambre succeeded because people wanted to be associated with his work. The ML experiment was backed by the CEO, and it was regularly coming up with unquestionable insights; the only way they could influence the ML—and have some of its success rub off on them—was to play by Mr. Dambre's rules.

In about two years, the knowledge created under the leadership of the MLs enabled Bekaert to achieve best-in-world performance in several areas. Moreover, during the 1991 recession, Bekaert withstood unbloodied most of the pummeling that its industry suffered. Ironically, outsiders refused to believe this remarkable story; one business journal attributed Bekaert's success to the ideas it supposedly had imported from its Japanese joint venture!

By the mid-1990s Bekaert decided to involve a key supplier (Thyssen) and a key customer (Pirelli) in its ML effort. By doing so, Bekaert and Pirelli would be able to sense and respond to material issues Thyssen could not control, while Thyssen would gain deeper insights into their real needs. To this end, Bekaert offered Thyssen and Pirelli access to its knowledge base and process. The partnership, however, did not last; culture is hard to transfer, and economic pressures kept Thyssen and Pirelli from emulating Bekaert effectively.

Create Self-Contained Learning Organizations

Successful businesses inevitably enter new markets, launch new products, and open new facilities. Executives should use such occasions to create learning organizations that are sheltered from the mainstream processes, organizations, and culture. The key challenge is finding leaders who can simultaneously manage business challenges and the needs of a learning organization.

In the base business, one possible solution is creating a "community of practice." This term describes a group of people who may be geographically, temporally, and organizationally dispersed, but who have a common interest. Such communities typically are informal and bypass formal organizational structures. They may spring up on their own and attract members largely through word of mouth. They usually are self-directed; the best adopt mores and values that enable them to acquire and share knowledge about their interests. They also adopt policies and processes to make this goal routine and effective. In other words, they are perfect learning organizations. The "memory core team" at HP, mentioned earlier, is a great example.

Just as the auto companies could not force RevCo to share its knowledge of possible failure modes, executives cannot force a community of practice into existence or drive its output. People join such communities because they want to, not because they have been forced to. So managers have to be willing to encourage the formation of such communities and give them the resources they need to thrive—time, collaboration technology and processes, the ability to meet face-to-face on occasion, and recognition. Then, they must sit back and hope that over time the company will benefit from the resultant collaboration. The managers' other challenge will be transferring knowledge created by these communities to those who need the knowledge, but who are not members. Overcoming this will require one or more of the other strategies described here.

Make Learning a Line Responsibility

During the heyday of the quality movement, a possibly apocryphal story was told about Xerox CEO Paul Allaire and Edward Deming, the doyen of quality. Struggling to survive against the onslaught of Japanese copiers, Xerox had to improve product quality. Mr. Deming advised Mr. Allaire to begin each management team meeting by asking about quality and *to leave the room after that discussion*. Nothing focuses the corporate mind—even at top levels—faster than the answer to the question "What does the CEO care about?" Xerox began taking quality seriously and lived to fight another day. If this story is not true, it should be! *It goes to the heart of managerial responsibility for creating any capability that is critical to a company's success.*

Most companies lay the responsibility for learning on employees. The oft-repeated logic for this policy is "We live in a 'Me, Inc.' world, and each person is responsible for remaining employable." *In the best-managed companies*, responsibility *also* lies with a training function that is typically housed within human resources. Training offers courses that employees—with the approval of their managers—can take to improve their own capabilities.

The problem is that even when a company offers training and its people participate, no one is responsible for ensuring that the engine of organizational learning (processes, structure, and culture) is producing the learning strategies the company needs. What a colossal waste of opportunity!

Companies must make individual managers stewards of the aspects of the learning engine that are in their bailiwicks. If not, they will have a hard time becoming *or remaining* adaptive. Managers must ensure that their people have the processes, structure, and culture that will enable their employees to actually use what they have learned on their own (private knowledge) or through training (semipublic knowledge).

Consider how Toyota makes its managers personally and directly responsible for enabling their staff to learn by providing the necessary processes, structure, and cultural scaffolding. Steven Spear wrote that one of the four lessons that Toyota managers learned is "Managers should coach, not fix." This lesson, he said, results in a "high degree of sophisticated problem solving at all levels of the organization." The training of a newly hired manager, he said, focused not on his own problem-solving skills, but on his ability to foster problem solving by workers and more junior managers. Moreover, the training did not tell the manager "what or how he was to learn." Indeed, the executive responsible for the training "positioned himself as a teacher and coach" and "at no point did he suggest actual...improvements." The executive did, however, give the new manager "the resources he needed to act quickly..."

There is no waste here, only world-beating competitive advantage. Half a world away, Nokia uses a very similar approach to buttress an equally powerful competitive advantage. Mr. Baril:

> We believe a lot in coaching. Coaching is asking open questions. I will help you to reflect, but not give you a solution. This is different from mentoring, where you give someone an answer.... Your superior won't tell you what you need to improve. You have to help yourself by finding out.

Change the Incentives

Professionals in performance management often say that to get people to behave differently, incentives that drive their behavior must be changed.[18] This insight should be used to promote learning at the individual, team, functional, and organizational levels. The actual steps will vary across organizations and depend on policies—or the absence thereof—that keep people from learning and improving therein. So people in each organization can best provide ideas about which incentives should change. The following list is merely meant to provoke thought:

- Institute awards for the most meaningful transfer of best practices *and* the most productive *copying* of best practices across teams and facilities.[19]
- Set training goals for every manager. Rate those who use their training budgets *fully and meaningfully* higher than those who do not.
- Reward managers for facilitating and guiding improvement *efforts*, not just for achieving numeric targets.
- Make the ability to coach and train staff—instead of simply directing them—a key requirement for promotions.

Often, it is possible to identify local changes in incentives that do not require major modifications in structure or process. This is particularly true since how people get evaluated changes regularly in most companies. So, introducing new policies may not foster opposition, particularly if some carrots are included in the mix. The small behavioral changes that result may ready people for other, more difficult modifications.

Final Thoughts

Building a learning organization takes time, particularly if a company has to undo years of policies that might have implicitly and unintentionally sabotaged learning. So, while it would be tempting to focus right from the start on cross-organizational learning—after all, Adaptive Businesses are all about working in networks—this is rarely a good idea. Grandiose plans to build learning capabilities that involve multiple organizations are risky because each has its own learning engine—culture, process, and organization. Such plans tend to succeed only if someone who has the power to move roadblocks—such as a CEO or a relatively autonomous head of a business unit—leads the charge.

The good news is that if each organization in a network focuses on becoming a learning organization in its own right, opportunities to build cross-organizational capabilities will naturally present themselves. Often they will arise simply from the realization, "I wish I had that data," and the recognition that a peer in a partner company might be able to help.

Finally, how can you tell whether a company is truly a learning organization? Ironically, companies that are learning organizations have a hard time recognizing themselves as such. Learning is so basic a value in them that they sometimes cannot even articulate what they do. Almost all of my interviewees at Nokia and HP struggled with the question. When I asked him a broad, open-ended question about the types of issues I have discussed here, Mr. Korhonen said, "We don't have very good institutionalized learning systems. But it is somehow in the DNA." Faced with the same question, Mr. Baril admitted, "We have never asked ourselves the question.... We do a lot of things in learning." He paused and hesitantly noted, with a question in his tone, "We have a Director of Developing People on the team?" Similarly, I suspect that most Toyota executives probably could not have specified the rules and lessons Mr. Spear used to characterize their learning engine but probably would have recognized them as formulated.

The definition I gave for organizational learning should be a good guide. Test your company against each of the elements of the definition, and if you honestly do well, you are a learning organization. If you do not, start worrying about your company's medium-term health, regardless of what the current financial numbers say. Head-to-head against a company that applies the third Design Principle of Adaptive Businesses, your company will be at a serious disadvantage.

So, You Are Not the CEO...

Early in this chapter, I called this Design Principle the "the ener-gizing spark that drives all aspects of adaptive behavior." Ironically, many mid-career executives do not apply it to organizational tinder even when they have the power to do so. Doing so simply requires a willingness to think creatively about what can be lit and the courage to actually do it.

You can build on the two challenges you identified earlier by focus-ing on work processes that will be affected. Work with your team to determine what the appropriate signals and analyses should be and what noise could confound your learning. Realign the process, cul-tural, and organizational context for your changes! If you cannot change the organization, consider what compensating mechanism you can put into place on your own.

More generally, take the following steps with your own team:

1. Cross-train your direct reports and, if possible, ask them to do the same with their staff. Broadening perspectives allows peo-ple to question whether they are simply holding on to nonex-istent horses.

2. Delegate every decision that you can. Coach your delegatees on how to make the decisions, keeping in mind Mr. Baril's distinction between coaching and mentoring.

3. Change your performance assessment approach to ensure that you credit people who learn something valuable from a bad situation—even one that they created.

4. Invest in training, and personally make sure that when your staff returns from training, they use what they learned.

5. Regularly assemble your team and review your work processes, *with a bias toward making changes*, instead of pre-serving the *status quo ante*.

6. Institute the Hewlett-Packard *post mortem* process.

Endnotes

[1]My definition is intentionally silent about a point that concerns many scholars: the use of acquired knowledge. Unlike a university, a company exists to make money. From its perspective, if what it learns cannot influence its available choices of action, this is not relevant knowledge.

[2]Here are more details on the selected books:

- *Organizational Learning: A Theory of Action Perspective*, by Chris Argyris and Donald A. Schon, Addison-Wesley, 1978.

- *The Fifth Discipline: The Art & Practice of the Learning Organization*, by Peter M. Senge, Currency, 2006 (originally published in 1990 by Doubleday Currency).

- *An Evolutionary Theory of Economic Change*, by Richard R. Nelson and Sidney G. Winter, Belknap Press, 2006 (originally published in 1982 by Harvard University Press).

- *Situated Learning: Legitimate Peripheral Participation*, by Jean Lave and Etienne Wenger, Cambridge University Press, 1991.

- *Essence of Decision: Explaining the Cuban Missile Crisis*, Second Edition, by Graham T. Allison, Longman, 1999 (originally published in 1971 by Little, Brown & Co.).

[3]In its most basic form, the learning (or experience) curve suggests that where repetitive work is done, unit cost of the output declines, often sharply, as the cumulative production volume rises.

[4]*The Effective Management of Organizational Learning and Process Control in Factories*, by Amit S. Mukherjee. A doctoral thesis submitted to the Harvard University Graduate School of Business Administration, 1992, available through Amazon.com and University Microfilm, Inc. The Harvard Business School and Bekaert cofunded the research. The document also contains an earlier version of Figure 6-1 and the two italicized arguments near the figure.

[5]My boss, Professor Luk Van Wassenhove, and Ph.D. student Michael Lapre (now an Associate Professor at Owen School of Business at Vanderbilt) brought skills that complemented mine.

[6]"Knowledge Driven Quality Improvement," by Amit S. Mukherjee, Michael Lapre, and Luk N. Van Wassenhove, *Management Science*, November 1998. "Behind the Learning Curve: Linking Learning Activities to Waste Reduction," by Michael Lapre, Amit S. Mukherjee, and Luk N. Van Wassenhove, *Management Science*, May 2000. "Learning Across Lines: The Secrets of More Efficient Factories," by Michael Lapre and Luk N. Van Wassenhove, *Harvard Business Review*, October 2002. Table 2-1 is adapted from similar tables in the last two publications.

[7]Peter Senge's "systems thinking"—building models of how a system (such as a business) works—is an example of conceptual knowledge/learning. "Personal mastery" *may* result from—and almost certainly embodies—experiential knowledge.

[8]Newton's theory of gravitation posits that an iron ball and a feather will accelerate equally rapidly while falling. Yet in the real world, this prediction is demonstrably untrue, because the atmosphere slows the feather sharply. The theory is correct, but it implicitly assumes a vacuum, a condition not normally found on Earth.

[9]"Decoding the DNA of the Toyota Production System," by S.J. Spear and H.K. Brown, *Harvard Business Review*, September–October 1999. "Learning to Lead at Toyota," S.J. Spear, *Harvard Business Review*, May 2004.

[10]I am assuming that the creation and use of knowledge meet the last element of my definition: ethical. If people exposed to these ideas are not already ethical, nothing I say will make them so.

[11]A well-used process satisfies Richard Nelson and Sidney Winter's conception of a "routine."

[12]*Reengineering the Corporation: A Manifesto for Business Revolution*, by Michael Hammer and James A. Champy, New York: Harper Collins, 2003 (originally published in 1993).

[13]This excerpt has been reprinted with permission. The reprinted material is from Etling E. Morison's *Men, Machines, and Modern Times* (excerpted from pages 17-44) published by the MIT Press.

[14]"Right triangular backstop" to an engineer is a triangle shaped block, with one 90° angle, used to stop something from sliding back. Professor Teboul would draw a triangle (with one of the two sides that make the 90° angle touching the stick figure) and write ISO 9000 on it.

[15]Doing so will build Argyris and Schon's Double Loop learning capability into work processes.

[16]Organizational structure and the third element, culture, play major roles in organizational decision-making, along the lines of Graham Allison's perspective on organization and culture.

[17]For example, Mr. Schneider's business unit was more willing than others to risk adopting an untested PRM approach.

[18]Undoubtedly some people, including many great leaders and top performers, are "self-actualized" and don't need incentives.

[19]For years, Nestlé gave its R&D centers around the globe budgets for people to travel to meet and get to know scientists in other centers. Nestlé felt that such socialization built the trust needed to teach and learn from those with whom one did not interact daily. While this policy may be impossible to implement in most companies today, it was a truly creative solution for "not invented here syndrome." And it was far better than policies that promote "My lab is better than your lab" attitudes.

7

Make Technology Matter

A few years ago, Forrester Research, one of the premier IT analyst firms in the world, hired me to build a strategy consulting practice from scratch. One early client was the CIO of a multibillion-dollar business group of one of the world's largest companies. She asked me to attend a meeting that her boss, the corporate CIO, had organized for the company's fifty-odd top IT executives around the world. She wanted me to bring Analyst B, who had recently written a very influential report about the implementation costs of a key corporate software ("Software").

While preparing for the meeting, I confirmed that B planned to tell the client that it should expect to spend about $2 billion over the next five years adopting Software. I then asked, "What do you think will be the very first question they will ask?" "I don't know," B replied. "I do," I said. "They'll say, 'B, can you prove that we will get greater value by spending $2 billion on Software than if we spent the same $2 billion to create a new product or license a new technology or enter a new market or even buy back our own shares?'" B looked at me shell-shocked before exploding, "How the hell am I supposed to know that? I'm a Software analyst!" I suggested that he think about the answer to that question prior to the meeting. He did not, and the first question posed to him matched mine almost word for word.

Another premier name among IT analyst firms is Gartner. Recently, I read some of the blogs on its website.[1] On March 31, 2006, Mark Raskino, a research vice president at Gartner, titled his post "Is

IT Out of Ideas?" In it he noted that Gartner's own surveys suggest "...a rather mediocre strategic investment attitude toward IT" and confessed, "...recently I have met some CIOs who suggest IT is not a business strategic force, while others say their primary objective is simply to cut the cost of IT to the company." Mr. Raskino continued:

> A cursory glance at IT industry umbrella marketing suggests some fuzziness. "Business agility" is vague, and few companies get passionate about ideas like "on-demand business" or "the adaptive enterprise." Compliance is sometimes seen as FUD [fear, uncertainty, doubt], and security is an operating cost. Web 2.0 looks like fun for Google and Silicon Valley start-ups—but not much else.

A few days later, Mr. Raskino added that a CIO from the plastics industry told him that "...he did not see IT as important to business innovation" and instead "...quickly became enthusiastic about a future where we all drink beer from plastic bottles instead of glass." Trying to answer Mr. Raskino, Gartner Fellow Martin Reynolds wrote, "One of the great IT challenges remains that of delivering on existing requirements and new projects in a timely and efficient fashion." To this, Mr. Raskino replied, "That's an interesting perspective, [Mr. Reynolds]. Without getting the basics right—why should IT be allowed to get involved in more business innovation?" I had no trouble imagining him shake his head in disbelief.

Others tried harder to soothe Mr. Raskino's furrowed brow. Another Gartner Fellow, Richard Hunter, cited the consulting company McKinsey to support his assertion that "scientific management" and "automation that changes the way managers...work" will be the next big thing. He acknowledged that scientific management harks back to the early twentieth century (it was Ramchandran Jaikumar's third of six epochs!), but he noted that "...there is certainly big untapped potential for IT to change how executives run the show." A sector vice president, Daryl Plummer, gently chided Mr. Raskino ("...witness the comment that 'agility' is vague...") before adding:

...we are shifting from a focus on the technologies that IT brings to the table, toward the things you can do with them to bring you value. This is a too-subtle shift for some to grasp...ideas like software as a service (SaaS), virtualization, mobile workforce, collaborative communities, IT utilities, service-oriented architecture (SOA), and even Web 2.0 all share at least one common trait—they lead us to center our attention on what we do, who we do it with, and what the value is, instead of the technology that makes it possible. That is the wave of the future.... It is about collaboration, it is about information, it is about processes, it is about people, and it is indeed about the effective, efficient use of technology to enable a desired outcome—agility.

I am not poking fun at Forrester or Gartner or any of their analysts. Forrester is a great analyst firm, and B was an excellent Software analyst. Forrester gave me the opportunity to create for it a business unit that added significant value for its clients. And though I quoted tongue-in-cheek from Gartner's blog, I applaud Mr. Raskino's courage for publicly raising the issue he did and Gartner management for allowing this debate to proceed in public.

Instead, I wanted to use the anecdotes to suggest that just as technology is affecting the most minute aspects of our work, those who study it for a living are struggling to understand how it fits—or should fit—into businesses. And that is why when someone like Nick Carr writes a book that coherently argues that "Technology doesn't matter," few can argue, equally coherently, why it does.[2]

We must do better, by adopting the perspective of a general manager. Kim Clark, a renowned expert on technology, articulated the first half of this perspective: "Technology without strategy gives no competitive advantage."[3] Technology partisans often do not understand this perspective. The CIOs of the global company challenged B for advocating Software as the one right answer for their company without knowing what corporate—or even functional—strategy Software would enable. The lack of passion that Mr. Raskino observed for the technology described as "on-demand" (by IBM) or "adaptive" (by SAP, HP, Sun, and others) is simply a broadening of B's error: technology partisans have not clearly articulated *why* businesses *must* get excited about these very powerful, potentially valuable, but admittedly very expensive tools.

It makes no sense to sell "collaboration" (like Mr. Plummer) or "scientific management" (like Mr. Hunter) or good project management (like Mr. Reynolds) or "the low cost of implementation and maintenance" (like most vendor websites). Neither individually nor collectively will they deliver competitive advantage.[4] Offered such "benefits," I too would—like the CIO of the plastics firm—wax eloquent about the wonders of plastic beer bottles; the opportunity to earn profits easily outranks the adoption of technology of unclear value.

I articulated the other half of the argument when I told Mr. Clark: "There are times in human history when strategy without technology also gives no competitive advantage." From this perspective, it would be silly for any company today to re-create Nokia's original telephone-and-spreadsheets-based sense-and-respond capabilities. Competitors could buy more sophisticated capabilities pretty much off the shelf and easily seize competitive advantage. The conceptually valid strategy would be inadequate without the backing of the latest technology.

Yet ironically, this is the mistake that many executives, including the plastic company's CIO, are making. They are tired of all the "Wolf! Wolf!" cries they have heard over the years. Dot-coms did not dismantle large companies (few industries outside the media are at risk), and where they took center stage (such as at AOL Time Warner), they brought nothing but trouble. So, they are applying the "mushroom cultivation principle" to technology: Lock it in a dark cellar, and throw manure on it, and something valuable *may* sprout over time.

In effect, advocates of technology are stuck on the "technology without strategy" side of the fence, while many executives are stuck on the "strategy without technology" side of the fence. They resemble an unhappily married couple that cannot figure out how to effect a divorce without one side slipping into poverty and the other side fearing being saddled with burdens, particularly financial, that it cannot afford. Yet this is not a dispute that anyone can lightly ignore: In early 2007, another technology analyst firm, IDC, concluded that worldwide spending on IT—hardware, software, and services—would rise from almost $1.2 *trillion* in 2006 to almost $1.5 trillion by 2010.[5]

The fourth Design Principle for Adaptive Businesses asks executives to embrace the marriage while jettisoning the baggage that is burdening it. It says, very simply, **Deploy technologies that enable intelligent adjustment to major environmental shifts.** Adaptive Businesses need four key capabilities from technologies: *Provide visibility, support analysis, facilitate collaboration*, and *enable mobility*. Conversely, without these four capabilities, it would be pretty hard to become adaptive. As such, these four groups of technologies should be the basis for the marriage of the business and technology. The critical corollary to the Principle is *Set very high thresholds for other technologies (unless they are required for security or regulatory mandates, or are essential for the routine running of the business), for they probably will not provide competitive advantage.*

Provide Visibility

Visibility is the ability to "see"—What do we have? How much do we have? Where is it? When will we have it?—into a company's internal and external environments. It not only gives you the ability to *sense* emerging problems and opportunities, but also provides the information that, if analyzed appropriately, enables the marshalling of cogent responses. Visibility technologies are the cornerstones of an Adaptive Business, because they enable the effective application of the first and third Design Principles. Their role is comparable to that of quality a few decades ago, when managers learned that better quality led to higher productivity, more innovation, and greater profits. Pertti Korhonen repeatedly emphasized the importance of visibility:

> For example, for [a key vendor] we could show one number [of] what we had from them in the entire company. They said no one of our competitors could do it. *That meant when something went wrong, we could see it.* Some of our competitors could detect a problem only when the purchase order was not filled.

> We had been in a situation of shortage for so long that we had developed the power to steal globally. We were many times *within one hour of no inventory globally*.... Normally companies look at inventory from each factory.... [Our] factories were showing the global inventory levels to their suppliers...

> [After the fire] people also learned that visibility at this level of detail is an asset. It reinforced the need to *operate globally*. It helped to cultivate the need and value to operate globally.

In 2000, what Nokia had was basic but crucial technology that gave it *visibility inside* its own boundaries: an Enterprise Resource Planning (ERP) system from a major vendor. Nothing fancy—and certainly, by then, an old idea for analysts of technology. That is why—as I wrote in Chapter 1, "The Fire That Changed an Industry"—technology played a key *supporting* role, and the role was "so prosaic that no technology partisan that I know ever wrote about it." Nokia gained a competitive advantage because it recognized that *global* deployment of this prosaic technology could give it competitive advantage and followed through. If it had not, the production planner who detected the problem would not have been able to do so.

Current and Emerging Visibility Technologies

Less than a decade later, several powerful new technologies are available to companies to augment those available in 2000, and more are on the way. These technologies will extend visibility beyond the organizational and technological boundaries of individual companies.

Perhaps the best developed is the Global Positioning System (GPS), which has powered the explosive growth of "shipment tracking" services available from couriers and mail carriers. Any car, train, aircraft, or ship equipped with a GPS transponder can be tracked precisely almost anywhere worldwide. The technology does have weaknesses; it can get disoriented in the canyons formed by tall buildings in a city's downtown, and it cannot look into buildings. New generations of the technology will address such weaknesses, while devices like GPS-equipped mobile phones will expand its use by adding capabilities (such as tracking people).[6] Anticipating significant growth in both business and consumer use of this technology (and being leery of relying on the U.S. Department of Defense satellites to process all GPS signals), the European Union hopes to deploy its own GPS capability, called Galileo, by 2011.

Far less widely used are capabilities based on technologies known by acronyms like XML, UDI, and SOAP. When multiple companies connect using these technologies, they serve as simultaneous translators and directories among them. This allows the companies to conduct business transactions on an automated or semiautomated basis regardless of the differences in their internal policies and work processes. Originally, these capabilities focused on one industry, which presumably made the translating and directory functions easier. Starting in late 2005, these industry-specific capabilities began converging, reflecting the trend toward the blurring of industry boundaries.

For example, in 2006, Nokia used such a capability, the RosettaNet, to purchase 300 *billion unique* components; this would be hard to plan and execute manually. More importantly for our purposes, it used the RosettaNet twice a day to poll its network about the network's ability to support its plans. In effect, Nokia senses and responds as it did in March 2000, but far more often—and usually semiautomatically. It is also building a similar capability to connect with its key customers. When completed, the two capabilities will give it visibility into the needs of its customers and the abilities of its suppliers.

RFID, first mentioned in Chapter 4, "Transform Everyday Work," is yet another visibility technology that is in the early stages of deployment. An RFID tag can theoretically be attached to individual units of a product, such as a can of Coke. Like mobile phones, "active" RFID tags repeatedly announce their presence to nearby sensors ("passive" tags work differently, but this distinction is irrelevant here). Akin to mobile phone towers, the sensors pick up and convey these signals to computers that can pinpoint the tag's temporal and spatial location. They also access any other information it transmits. Such information can give a company unique ability to see into its environment and react to changes.

For example, suppose Wal-Mart's Store A faces very high demand for a product, while Store B does not. Informed in real time of declining inventories by its RFID system, Store A's management can request additional deliveries (perhaps semiautomatically or automatically). The warehouse can sense that Store B has enough inventory and can divert a supply truck meant for Store B to Store A. This capability, which Wal-Mart actually began building some time ago, is in effect a dramatically souped-up version of HP's Buy-Sell process. In the years ahead, software agents technology (also introduced in Chapter 4) will also automate the ordering and diversion decisions and speed up the process even more.

Making Strategic Decisions on Visibility

Concerns about costs have held back the full deployment of visibility technologies. Many companies do not even have truly global ERP (or similar) systems, and most small firms eschew capabilities like the RosettaNet. Businesses have been spending heavily on RFID since 2003, when Wal-Mart ordered all its major suppliers to become RFID-compliant by January 2005. But they have not done enough. In

December 2004, the technology analyst firm AMR wrote that Wal-Mart's suppliers had collectively spent $250 million on basic RFID technologies to date, and most had not seen positive returns.[7] AMR estimated that a collective investment of *$1.8 billion* would be needed for strategic impact. In mid-2005, AMR interviewed five hundred U.S. companies about their RFID plans.[8] Sixty-nine percent reported that *that year*, they intended to evaluate or pilot or implement or use RFID systems, though only eight percent expected it to be fully implemented. Twenty-eight percent expressed concern that they would not achieve acceptable returns on investment, but they had, on average, budgeted $550,000. AMR expected the budget to rise to $770,000 in 2007.

When such costs are externally mandated by powerful outsiders like Wal-Mart and the U.S. government, companies grumble about the cost and the enormity of the task. Sometimes they can get the mandates relaxed (as they did with Wal-Mart). But even then they focus single-mindedly on satisfying the mandates at the lowest possible cost. *As such, instead of improving visibility and sense-and-respond capabilities, they graft the mandated technologies onto their existing, inflexible plan-and-execute operations.*

A cursory review of articles shows that in the case of RFID, companies have defaulted to seeking answers to tactical questions like "Should we use active or passive tags?", "Should the sensor system be based in the warehouse or the factory?", and "What database system do we need?" *These are important questions, but not strategic ones.* By not pursuing their own strategic investigations, companies risk losing significant competitive advantage. In the case of RFID, for example, *the suppliers who were simply following Wal-Mart's mandates were unilaterally handing over technology-driven power to the one company that already held enormous power over their fortunes!* In the future, they will be even more at Wal-Mart's beck and call than they have been in the past.

In the near future, two key developments will change the business landscape. First, *technologies that enable sight within companies* (like RosettaNet and RFID) *will achieve the sophistication of (improved) GPS technology.* (Today, the technologies still have some important failings; for example, RFID tags cost more than had been anticipated and cannot be read consistently if placed next to metal.) Second, *all of these technologies will get interconnected*, so GPS, RFID, ERP, and RosettaNet-like networks will work in concert. Clearly, linking all such technologies into a digital technology network could dramatically improve visibility beyond the capabilities of the individual technologies.

These technologies will then be able to handle the trends toward decomposition of work, extreme customization, and the blurring of industries. They will provide far greater sense-and-respond capabilities than at present and as such will be able to power hard-to-surmount competitive advantage. At that point, two policy issues discussed in Chapter 4 will determine who will actually benefit from these developments. These two issues are cooperation among the various companies that will control the hardware, software, and data (the adoption of the second Design Principle) and societal attitudes about the privacy questions raised by technologies.

So how should companies make decisions about visibility technologies? Senior executives should authorize their use not because they have to, but because these technologies are powerful enough to affect strategy. They must ask questions like these:

- What do we *need* to know (not what would be nice to know)? Why?
- How will we get access to the information?
- How much is this information worth to us? How much are we willing to spend to get it?
- What will we actually be able to do with the information once we get it? What new response options will we have? How will we assess which one is better?

- If we do acquire the information, what strategic, infrastructural, and process changes will make us better able to respond *intelligently* and *with less effort*? Are we willing to—and able to—make these changes? (If not, don't waste money!)

- How much technology must our visibility system incorporate? Why? How do we know we will be safe at this level? What criteria will we use to decide when an emerging technology is good enough to be adopted?

- What risks do we run if we take these steps? What risks do we run if we *don't* take these steps? How will we mitigate them? For example, what is our bridge from what we can do today to what we really want to do?

- How should we train our people to use the information?

Support Analysis

Technologies for analysis look for patterns and anomalies in data. They often compare data against formal models or against older data sets in the company's organizational memory. These technologies are critical enablers of the first and third Design Principles.

Beginning in the early 1990s, analytical technologies usually were prepackaged into functional software. Each package contained the means to collect and analyze whatever data vendors (or IT consultants) thought their clients should have about the function. In recent years, the very structure of these technologies has begun changing. Software vendors now appreciate that in real life, problems often are not function-specific. Customer-facing software may pinpoint an opportunity to sharply increase sales by targeting specific customers. But to exploit that opportunity, the supply management software must ensure that sufficient quantities can be produced, and the finance and human resources software must ensure that the necessary resources are available.

So vendors began offering freestanding analytical tools, applicable across functions. These fall into three (roughly generational) categories:

- **Well-defined software to analyze stored data.**   This kind of software helps executives understand trends and status, perhaps by reporting them on "executive dashboards." Such software addresses issues known to be important, and the data it relies on generally is "clean." However, it is hard to use it to do spur-of-the-moment analyses, even on important issues.

- **Plug-and-play analysis software.**   This newer kind of software has built-in capabilities that allow it to connect easily to (some part of) any process in order to collect and analyze associated data. Such general-purpose analytical capability enables quick problem identification, localization, and solution. However, data collected in this fashion rarely is "clean" or accurate.

- **Real-time deep-analysis software.**   Most recently, software that enables the combining of historical data with the capturing of real-time data has begun appearing. Moreover, these software can increasingly understand analytical commands delivered in normal languages.

Thus, in the near future, analytical software could give individual managers and staff ready access to data and analyses that can corroborate or refute opinions or hunches. *This can help move discussion and decision-making from the realm of firefighting and routinized knowledge to the realm of empiricalized knowledge.* For example, had such capabilities been available to Paul Dambre at Bekaert (see the sidebar "Creating a Learning Organization: The Model Lines of Bekaert" in Chapter 6, "Ensure That Work Teaches"), he would not have had to shut down the senior manager who expressed an unsupported opinion. Instead, he could have immediately analyzed historical and real-time data to either corroborate or discredit the manager's opinion.

There is, however, no free lunch. At a perfunctory level, it is clear that to acquire such capabilities, companies must make major preparatory investments. For example, the marketing data may be stored in a different database and in a different form than supply chain data. Besides, what marketing calls a "feature" will inevitably be very different from the description manufacturing needs to make the "feature"; each needs its own jargon to do its own work. So, companies also have to invest in technologies that can communicate across multiple jargons.

At a much deeper level, these technologies can do great harm if they are deployed and used without adequate thought (such as if companies fall on the "technology without strategy" side of the fence). Three shortcomings can be particularly problematic:

- **The pursuit of empiricalized knowledge leads to intellectualized knowledge.**   Models embedded in (or created for) analysis are just that: models. They approximate reality and can help make sense of the world, but they are not reality and are not the real world. Unquestioning reliance on these—such as on executive dashboards—can lead people away from empiricalized knowledge and into the realm of intellectualized knowledge.

- **Data availability determines which problems receive attention.**   Sometimes we need tools that can help find a friend known to be living in one of the many apartments in a building. At other times, we need tools to determine whether anyone in the building is a friend. Most analytical technologies address the first type of problem. This bias makes them better at working with a targeted set of problems or opportunities than at uncovering the set of problems or opportunities that the company should target.

- **The organization is too biased toward action.**   Access to real-time or near-real-time knowledge can create an unnecessary bias toward intervention. All natural and people-made processes vary, even when they are performing exactly as designed. By responding instantaneously to changes they observe in data, companies can destabilize their networks.

Facilitate Collaboration

As a teenager, I read Ayn Rand's *The Fountainhead*. Rand's description of the solitary architect, in complete control of every aspect of the design and construction of a building, captivated me. Only after I became an academic researcher and a leader of two "next-generation" product-development projects did I realize the surreality of her worldview. For example, no single person could possibly master the range of disciplines needed to design a modern airliner, including engine design, aerodynamics, material science, electronics, ergonomics, control systems, and user interface design. In all fields of human activity, not just design, anything more than the simplest work requires *collaboration among individuals* with diverse knowledge, skills, and experiences. As work fragments across time and space, it also requires *collaboration among groups*. Technologies that enable such collaboration are critical for all of the prior three Design Principles.

In March 2000, Nokia used the standard collaboration tools of the day found in almost all product-driven companies. Computer-Aided Design (CAD), Computer-Aided Engineering (CAE), and Computer-Aided Manufacturing (CAM) software enabled it to re-design the chips and products affected by the fire and transmit these to its partners. The partners used the same tools to negotiate the changes that would make the new plans implementable. Today, Nokia also uses a web-based system to support many other types of people-to-people interactions with its partners. HP also enables collaboration with relatively simple and commonly available Internet-based tools; these, in fact, form the technical backbone of the Buy-Sell system.

As the data from my North American survey on behalf of SAP shows (see Figure 7-1), in 2003, companies that made products felt the need to collaborate across multiple tasks. A Yankee Group survey in 2006 confirmed and extended this assessment to a broader range of activities, including the customer-facing side, as shown in Figure 7-2.[9] (Though this study surveyed fewer companies [68], it included

nonmanufacturing businesses [43%] and also covered a broader
geography—North and Latin America, Europe, and Asia-Pacific.)

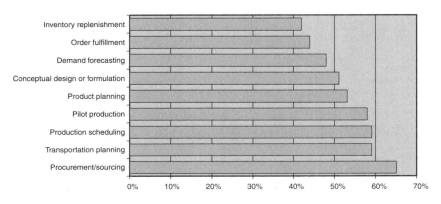

Source: SAP

Figure 7-1   Collaboration with peers in and outside the company.

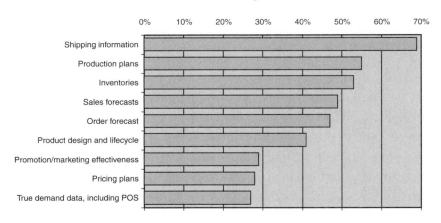

Source: Yankee Group

Figure 7-2   The extent of current or planned information sharing, 2007.

Reflecting this need, by 2003, software vendors had embedded
basic collaboration capabilities into most modern enterprise software
(such as ERP and CRM). The data from my survey confirmed the

widespread availability of these technologies (see Figure 7-3); 53% of the companies possessed even the least-used (Product Lifecycle Management [PLM], critical for engineers). Nevertheless, the more-basic technologies, e-mail and intranets, dwarfed the presence of the more high-tech capabilities.

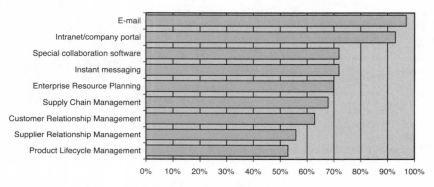

Figure 7-3   The availability of collaboration capabilities through standard technologies.

As the parent of a young horsewoman, I can personally attest to the veracity of the adage that you can lead a horse to water, but you cannot make it drink. People really are similar: they will not use collaboration capabilities just because they have access to them. As shown in Figure 7-4, half the companies I surveyed reported relatively low use of the *embedded* capabilities to collaborate with people within their companies and with partners. Moreover, people used all the tools internally far more frequently than they did externally and simpler tools far more often than sophisticated tools.

One reasonable explanation for this pattern might be that in 2003, the technologies still were not user-friendly. Another reason might be the difficulty of changing human behavior; as young, tech-savvy people become the mainstay of the workforce, face-to-face meetings, phones, faxes, and e-mails may well fall out of fashion. These may ex-plain why sophisticated technologies are less used, but not why, in a world of fragmented work (about 67% reported outsourcing levels at least as high as in the years past), usage of internal communications far exceeded usage of external ones. A third explanation can possibly ad-dress this shortcoming: people have not changed their *work patterns* as much as they should have.

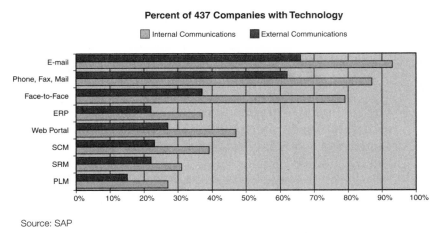

Source: SAP

Figure 7-4   Frequency of use of collaboration tools within and across companies.

Recently, even more powerful—and more user-friendly—collab-oration tools have become broadly available. These enable members of a group (say, a community of practice) to jointly work on issues. They can enter and exit virtual chat rooms to exchange views when they wish; no central authority must drive their participation. They can incrementally and continually update their understanding of com-plex issues by using "wiki" tools to modify each others' ideas; such a democracy of ideas ensures that no one has to centrally maintain the integrity of the collective knowledge. They can write blogs to express their opinions or answer questions and have others respond to them. They can hold low-cost videoconferences and webinars. They can verbally annotate—or even attach a video clip to—a piece of conceptual knowledge that requires experiential knowledge to work; they do not have to reduce it to a formal, explicit form.

As in the case of visibility technologies, analysts expect businesses to spend huge amounts of money on collaboration technologies. Ovum/Datamonitor expects the market for *advanced* collaboration tools (such as those just mentioned) will rise from $1 billion in 2005 to $1.7 billion in 2010.[10] The larger market for all collaboration tools will grow more slowly, from $2.4 billion to $2.7 billion.

Given these anticipated levels of spending, some executive in every company had better care deeply about technologies that facilitate collaboration! This executive should do the following:

- **Push people to experiment with new technologies instead of defaulting to old habits.**   New collaboration technologies, though not all, can speed up and/or improve decision-making. For example, by giving users simultaneous access to relevant information while they are interacting, technologies embedded in enterprise software can reduce the incidences of "I'll have to get back to you on that" and/or decisions based on misinformation. *But...*

- **Provide collaboration technologies that people want to use.**   *Once people have actually tried a new technology*, they, not "experts," should decide its fate. The company should support their choices if possible and eliminate technologies that do not engender enthusiasm.

  Knowledge management software offers a perfect example of the consequences of ignoring this recommendation. It seduced many managers into believing that they could capture their people's knowledge. Yet, such efforts were destined to fail! The software could capture conceptual knowledge but not routinized or empiricalized knowledge. It required someone to formally maintain the *Integrity of the Knowledge Base* (imagine this spoken in a loud, sonorous voice), and *potential users did not see any obvious benefits to the codification of their knowledge*. Theoretical promise clashed with lack of tangible benefit, and theory lost. *So...*

- **Tell IT to make it happen.**   When people identify technologies that they will use *and* these provide value, ensure that nothing impedes adoption. Collaboration, by definition, requires some degree of openness. Valid arguments against the technologies' deployment—such as "Our security will be compromised"—will arise. The decision bias should strongly favor deployment ("Figure out how to make it safe").

Enable Mobility

Researchers typically classify people as "mobile workers" if they spend at least 20% to 25% of their time (or one day a week) away from their primary workplace. All over the world, the proportion of people so classified has been rising. The best data is available for the European Union (EU), based on a 2005 survey of 30,000 people in 31 countries.[11] There, almost 30% of people work away from their home and offices at least 25% of the time. Estimates for the U.S., available from several sources, are difficult to reconcile because of differences in survey methodologies, definitions, and presentation of results. Nevertheless, they tend to range from 30% to 40%.[12, 13, 14] Additionally, the RAND Corporation study "The 21st Century at Work" cited primary research that found that 80% of the workforce either worked offsite or worked with others who did![15] In Asia, the levels of mobile workers are not yet comparable to those in the U.S. and Europe; 9% of the workforce of small and medium-sized businesses are mobile in China, and 10% are in India.[16]

Under the circumstances, mobility technologies, quintessential examples of distributed computer networks and the Johnny-come-lately tools to the adaptive party, will have a huge impact on companies and society at large. Their power can be attributed to their ability to enable people to work while they are on the move.

Simplistically, mobile technologies give people on the move two overlapping capabilities: the capability to *communicate with their primary places of work*, and the capability to *acquire information where they are and to manipulate or disseminate it as needed.* The increasingly ubiquitous personal digital assistants (PDAs) (of BlackBerry fame) belong to the first category. These technologies by and large increase their users' productivity. A recent Yankee Group survey, shown in Figure 7-5, suggests that strong pluralities of companies are currently planning on giving their staff such capabilities.[17]

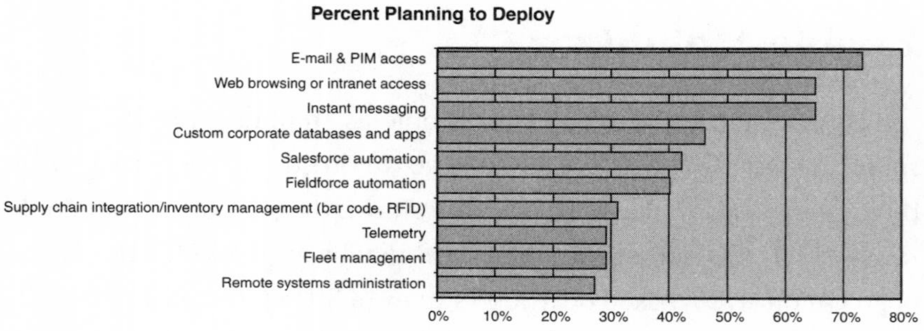

Percent Planning to Deploy

Source: Yankee Group

Figure 7-5   Corporate plans to deploy software applications for mobile workers, 2006.

The second category, I believe, will see explosive growth. Here, information is not just accessed or responded to, but is actually created *in situ,* either because it is best created there or because it may be difficult to create elsewhere. These technologies not only improve their users' productivity but, more importantly, may sharply improve the quality of work done. At the simplest end, in this category are devices like the ones FedEx drivers carry to record the pickup or delivery of packages. In the consumer sector, services like OnStar allow drivers to seek assistance on issues ranging from the location of the nearest restaurant to an overheating engine. Less common are devices that help technicians conduct field maintenance on expensive equipment by plugging a computer into the equipment and running a diagnostic. At an emerging level are devices that doctors can use to manage their care of patients at their hospital bedsides.

Taken together, the two categories of technologies will make it easier for companies to sense the unusual far from home. They will also enable spur-of-the-moment collaboration while people are away from traditional work spaces. Finally, by enabling real-time observation and documentation of events, they may make it easier for people and companies to learn. As such, they will support all the prior Design Principles.

Introducing mobility technologies, however, may be particularly difficult. Concerns about security will be a lot harder to dismiss outright. Users will constantly demand smaller, lighter, easier-to-connect devices. As manufacturers reduce size and weight to meet users' needs, these devices will be more likely to be stolen. A stolen, unprotected device in hostile hands may endanger critical data or a company's very functioning. New approaches to security—like biometric switches that disable devices being used by unauthorized people—will become common to counter such threats. However, as in all arms races, this will precipitate many years of one-upmanship between the white hats and black hats. There are no easy answers here; in contrast to the case of collaboration technologies, the advice of IT and security experts must be given considerable deference, and this may slow down technology adoption.

At a deeper level, *the deployment of mobile technologies will be challenging because they must be highly intertwined with other technologies.* While mobile workers can extend the visibility of their companies beyond their formal boundaries, to be effective, they need visibility into key issues within their companies and into their partner companies. For example, a technician cannot make a credible promise to get a piece of equipment working properly by a particular time unless he or she knows that the needed components are available. A substantial amount of visibility technology must be in place before mobility technologies can add value. Moreover, the ability to analyze information and learn on-the-fly and the ability to collaborate with peers will be just as important as having a mobile employee in place, providing information that can enable better analysis and the collaborative deployment of responses. Introducing mobile technologies not on an *ad hoc* basis, but as part of a custom package of tools, will be a key managerial challenge.

Implementing Adaptive Technologies

In effect, technologies that provide visibility, support analysis, facilitate collaboration, and enable mobility go hand-in-hand with an Adaptive Business approach to managing a company. Each of these capabilities facilitates intelligent adjustment to changed environmental conditions by allowing companies to detect such changes, analyze them, respond to them through collaborative action, and learn and disseminate what they have learned. Figure 7-6 summarizes these ideas; the directions of the arrows show the key links.

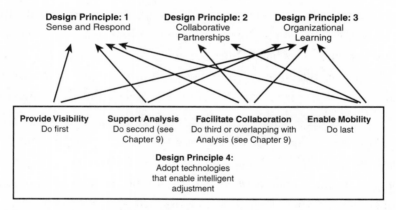

Figure 7-6   Links among the Design Principles.

It is also important to recognize what Figure 7-6 does *not* say. It does not say that the sense-and-respond capability must be embedded in plan and execute, nor how the collaborative partnerships can come about, nor how to ensure that people actually do learn in ways that benefit the company. *Technology can play a key role, but the fourth Design Principle, in and of itself, cannot make up for the absence of the first three.*

How, then, should executives go about implementing the fourth Design Principle? Five actions are critical.

Consider Capabilities Before Selecting Technologies

If asked, most executives say that they do SWOT (Strengths, Weaknesses, Opportunities, Threats) analysis by first defining their strengths and weaknesses and then evaluating opportunities and threats. This sequence leads to analyses that at best add no value and at worst endanger their companies. It biases their minds, making it more likely that they look at the external world through the lens of their own perceived capabilities. Because most people overestimate their own strengths and underestimate their weaknesses, this makes them more likely to miss great opportunities or critical threats. People doing SWOT should reverse the steps and evaluate external threats and opportunities before assessing the company's strengths and weaknesses vis-à-vis these challenges.

Similarly, to ensure coherence between strategy and technology, executives must *first* specify exactly *why* the four capabilities—visibility, analysis, collaboration, and mobility—will deliver competitive advantage. Only then should they address *how* they will *provide* visibility, *support* analysis, *facilitate* collaboration, and *enable* mobility—that is, select specific technologies. Too often companies either reverse these steps or ignore the capabilities analysis. By focusing on the technological features they have acquired, not on the strategic capabilities they need, they could find themselves unable to adapt to the market's dynamism.

A practical way of ensuring that this change of mind-set actually happens is changing how traditional return on investment (or net present value [NPV] or internal rate of return) analyses are done. Instead of determining the NPV of a new investment, people should first determine the financial benefits of a capability of interest (such as visibility into a partner's available capacity), if it could be achieved. Then they should determine the *maximum* investment that could give them a positive NPV for those benefits and look for appropriate technologies. Such an approach would truly focus technology investment decisions on strategic needs.

Focus on People

When companies implement new technologies or new processes, their cost-benefit analyses focus on the *business*. Implicitly, these analyses treat people as cogs, important only because their elimination often justifies the implementation. From Graham Allison's perspective (see Chapter 6), they assume rationality and ignore organizational and political drivers of choice and action. *Information* technology must incorporate all three drivers, because IT is the quintessential "experience good," whose value often cannot be discerned without use. A good IT tool may not create value because people do not use it, whereas an ordinary IT tool may become indispensable if users decide that it is good enough.[18]

Mr. Korhonen articulated this people-technology link, saying, "Tools can be brilliant, but they can't affect the behavior and decision-making of people." Early during Nokia's transformation, he focused on ensuring that the deployed technologies would be used:

> The key thing was that we did not go into information system in the beginning. We did not say, "Is there a solution? Can we buy i2 or SAP planning tools?" *It has to happen between the ears of the people. We have to rebuild the planning logic there.* We started with the people and, in the end, automated.

Today, Nokia is struggling with the fact this viewpoint is not broadly shared, even among the other companies it works with. Referring to the RosettaNet, Tapio Markki noted that people "...become too used to automated systems..." and their actions compromise their benefits. Sometimes, they take "...days ...to react" to plans that the systems say are feasible. Nokia's solution has been to turn back to people.

While its plan-and-execute capabilities continue to get as automated as possible, human beings still oversee the (automated) sense-and-respond capabilities. In Jean-Francois Baril's words, this means "...we need to keep human intervention for dealing with exceptions detected by the systems, and business judgment."

Smart machines, sociologist Shoshana Zuboff's provocative term for computers, then, are only as good as the humans who work with them. Defining what people *should* do with them and tracking what they are *actually* doing with them must be a key managerial responsibility. Such oversight can actually lead to better use of better technology.

Avoid Band-Aids and Artistic Flourishes

When companies introduce new technologies, they often graft features and work-arounds onto their existing technologies and processes. Some of this is unavoidable; if every technology adoption had to begin with a "clean sheet of paper," many companies would go bankrupt. However, excessive grafting can make a technology unwieldy enough to constrain the very capabilities being sought. Mr. Baril drew an engineering analogy to make this case:

> If you add and patch your core technology asset, you will fail. This is where [most well-established firms] go wrong.... You have to worry about the architecture, and *at one point, you have to architect the technology differently*. If I am a baseband designer, I can't just think of how I can modify the baseband. If I am a GPS designer, I can't just think of what features to add.... At some point I need to redesign the entire engine.

In an earlier chapter, I quoted Mr. Korhonen making a similar point. He had warned that if it is coupled with *functional- or departmental-level* continuous-improvement efforts, technology only cements suboptimal work processes into place. Redesigning the *cross-functional or cross-departmental* work flows (that is, Mr. Baril's "architecture") is a crucial first step.

HP's Venu Nagali worried about the opposite problem—that of complexity. While starting with a clean sheet of paper makes it possible to satisfy everyone's wish list, doing so can allow new bugs to creep in, costs to rise, and time lines to slip; better most definitely becomes the enemy of good. Mr. Nagali spoke of creating the PRM software (which, in this chapter's taxonomy, supports analysis and facilitates collaboration):

> We decided to keep software simple, not to make the software feature-rich. Why? Because, if so, you make it a daunting challenge for the other side, the users.... We have [also] stayed away from customizing. Our goal is, keep it simple, and solve 80% of the problem.

The combined lesson of these seemingly contradictory views is, start with a clean sheet of paper if possible, but in these cases, temper your goals with a healthy dose of realism. In the end, a little adaptive capability that works is better than a lot that does not.

Include a Mix of People on the Team

As recently as 2002–2003, on advice from their consultants and analysts, many companies were using stand-alone, full-time "tiger teams" for many IT projects. Their choice ignored the lesson that R&D and quality organizations learned during the late 1980s: companies often resisted innovations, no matter how valuable, developed by such teams, unless they were superbly connected to their parent organizations. IT projects could have been more effective if they had sought the advice of a few old-timers! In contrast, if I had to lead a technology project today, I too would have a set of blinders on. I would be handicapped by my lack of extensive experience with playing online games or participating in online communities, so I would be well served by having on my team people who use these technologies daily.

The importance of diversity in an adaptive technology effort cannot be understated. IT consultants and analysts keep extolling the virtues of "business sponsorship," but this recommendation, while necessary, is wholly inadequate. Teams, including sponsors, *must* include people of different ages, skill sets, and experiences; including technology cynics (as long as they are not Luddites) who can force teams to think broadly and creatively. Indeed, the critical error would be leaving such work to "experts." Mr. Baril, an engineer with two master's degrees in engineering, noted that if technology "...is driven only by technical people, it will fail. The engineer's mind-set might be sometimes too analytical." Creative leadership by "real people" is preferable to purely technical leadership or business leadership of technical personnel.

Remember Richard Feynman

Nobel laureate Richard Feynman, a physicist, served on the commission that investigated the *Challenger* space shuttle disaster. The *Challenger* exploded when a rubber ring that separated the gases that powered the rocket engine from the combustion chamber failed. Project staff reported to the commission that they had agonized for hours over whether the unusually cool weather (in the low 30s Fahrenheit) could cause failure, but their data was wildly contradictory. Feynman asked an aide to mix drinking water and tap water in a glass until it achieved the right temperature, and he dipped into it a piece of the same type of rubber. A short while later, the rubber became brittle. Case closed.

IT projects, like most major technical endeavors, are often fraught with uncertainties and complexities. Project teams try to obviate their impact by committing huge amounts of resources. They complain about corporate mandates that limit innovations that could help resolve the issues—or, conversely, they impose protective mandates that end up impeding innovations by others. Efforts to build adaptive capabilities can exacerbate such challenges, because they may require many novel steps.

In such situations, Feynman's lesson can help: *If a problem is complex or shrouded in uncertainty, before acting, design an empirical test that clarifies the core issues.* Don't create a sophisticated system to provide visibility when needed without first bench-testing it. Don't assume that the latest technology will facilitate collaboration or support analysis; actually observe how people use it. Ignore arguments about why such tests can't be done, don't make sense, or won't give useful results. If it is impossible to design a simple test of the core ideas, it will probably be impossible to design complex technologies to work on those ideas.

Final Thoughts

In past epochs, companies had to change themselves to take advantage of the capabilities of the new technologies. (For example, to effectively use SPC charts, they had to adopt team-based problem solving.) *In contrast, distributed computer networks not only are forcing change on companies, but also are rapidly evolving as companies adopt them and modify their work practices, structure, and values.* The tools for visibility, collaboration, analysis, and mobility will improve sensing and responding, collaborative action, and learning—but will also affect the continued decomposition of work, the ability to serve markets of one, and the blurring of industries.

So, organizational change and technological change have become the two halves of a self-reinforcing cycle. To build adaptive capabilities, companies must adopt appropriate technologies. To use adaptive technologies effectively, companies must adopt adaptive capabilities. The "technology without strategy" argument is bumping up hard against the "strategy without technology" argument. There is no way forward, except by embracing both arguments.

So, You Are Not the CEO...

The five ideas on implementing technologies should help all managers and professionals. A broader question is, are *you* ready to deal with the technological demands of an epoch being driven by distributed computer networks?

Today, it is hard to cite any personal (excluding intrinsically human) or business activity that is untouched by information technologies. Under the circumstances, you cannot abdicate responsibility for *understanding* IT. The lack of such understanding, I believe, has more than a passing impact on the inability of executives, analysts, and consultants to marry *the strategy without technology argument* to *the technology without strategy argument*.

Ideally, you should seek out some direct, hands-on experience with IT and/or its management. You do not have to learn to write code or even know what the acronym SOAP means. You do have to know enough to ask hard questions about whether, how, why, and when a technology can help your business become adaptive. More importantly, you must be able to credibly ask, "Why not?" when an expert says, "It can't be done." If you can't ask this question, you will not be able to marry strategy and technology to create unique capabilities.

At the very least, you should do the following:

1. Regularly read the technology section of a *general-purpose* media (such as *The New York Times'* "Science Times" and "Circuits" sections) so that you understand how technology interacts with culture, politics, business, and the economy. IT-focused publications are too enamored with technology *per se* to give you this broad perspective; use them judiciously to augment your knowledge.

2. Volunteer for project teams working on initiatives with technology components. Do not be shy about asking questions. It is better to *appear* uninformed in those circumstances than *be* uninformed when you have to make a multimillion-dollar decision alone.

Endnotes

[1]*Does IT Risk Boring Business?* http://blog.gartner.com/blog/unconthink.php.

[2]*Does IT Matter? Information Technology and the Corrosion of Competitive Advantage*, Nicholas Carr, Boston: Harvard Business School Publishing Corporation, 2004.

[3]Kim Clark is the former dean of the Harvard Business School and was a member of my doctoral thesis committee. He may actually have written these words in some article; if so, I do not recall where.

[4]Collaboration, *as I have defined it*, is vitally important for Adaptive Businesses.

[5]IDC, "Worldwide IT Spending, 2006–2010 Forecast Update by Vertical Market: North America, West Europe, Asia Pacific, and Rest of World," IDC #205018.

[6]"New TV Tracking Technology Goes Beyond GPS," by Dean Takahashi, *Sydney Morning Herald*, May 27, 2005.

[7]"AMR Research Finds Wal-Mart Suppliers Spent Only Minimum Required to Comply with RFID Mandate," AMR Research press release, December 20, 2004.

[8]"2005: A Pivotal Year for RFID Evaluation—Now Show Me the ROI" by Marianne D'Aquila, Dennis Gaughan, *AMR Research*, July 29, 2005.

[9]The Yankee Group, "Employing a Multi Supply Chain Strategy for Supply Chain Collaboration," January 2, 2007.

[10]"Collaboration: Communication on Steroids," by Angela Eager, *Computer Business Review Online*, May 3, 2007.

[11]"Fourth European Working Conditions Survey," by Agnès Parent-Thirion, Enrique Fernández Macías, John Hurley, and Greet Vermeylen, the EU Foundation for Improvement of Living and Working Conditions, 2007.

[12]The Yankee Group, "The Mobile Workforce: How Enterprises Must Adapt to Survive," August 4, 2006.

[13]"Germany Pulls Back, Netherlands, France and Austria Surge," by Sether Ross, *Broadband Properties*, March 2006.

[14]"Worldwide Mobile Worker Population 2005–2009, Forecast and Analysis, IDC #34124, October 2005, cited in IDC white paper for iPass, "Convenience, Security and Manageability: How to Make Mobile Workforce Programs Most Effective," October 2006.

[15]"The 21st Century at Work: The Forces Shaping the Future Workforce and Workplace in the United States," by Lynn Karoly and Constantjin Panis, RAND Corporation, Santa Monica, Calif., 2004.

[16]"China's SMBs to up Mobile Investments," by Lynn Tan, *ZDNet Asia*, May 7, 2007.

[17]The Yankee Group, "Enterprise Mobility Is the Last Mile in Must Adapt to Survive," August 4, 2006.

[18]I acquired a wonderful example of this fact while consulting with a company that provides technologies for traders in financial institutions. Once traders get used to a particular type of technology, they resist modifications—including new/improved features and simplified operations—whose incorporation requires changes in how they work. For example, when my client added drop-down menus, a boon to most people, it had to retain the old means of data entry *equally prominently*. So, it is easier to sell such technologies to companies that do not have them than to upgrade technologies that are already in place.

Part III

Going Adaptive

"You are never given a wish without also being given the power to make it true. You may have to work for it, however."

—Richard Bach, *Illusions*

8

Create the Organization

In the fall of 1997, I attended the joint franchisee convention for Dunkin' Donuts and Baskin-Robbins, two brands that are owned by one of the world's largest chain restaurant companies. As I sat in a cavernous auditorium in a Disney World hotel, Bill Rosenberg, who had founded Dunkin' Donuts, shuffled onto the stage. He was frail, probably well into his eighties; yet his strong voice belied his appearance as he said, "People don't build businesses. People build organizations, and organizations build businesses." The profoundness of Mr. Rosenberg's insight brings me to the issue of organization design, for companies must rethink their organizations so that they can actually build great businesses in this new epoch.

Earlier in this book, I noted (see, in particular, Table 3-1) that Ramchandran Jaikumar's research showed that with each epochal change, the following happened:

- **Work got transformed.** In the present epoch, this is taking the form of fragmentation of work across time and space. The fragmentation has given rise to the need to embed sense-and-respond capabilities in normal plan-and-execute processes and to foster collaborative action with network partners.

- **Consistent with the changes in work, skills and capabilities valued by companies evolved.** In this epoch, the importance of *learning* is very high due to the need to collect and process vast amounts of information that may enable sensing and responding. In addition, people must be able to *generalize* their insights beyond their own work areas and be willing and able to *share* these with other partners who might benefit from them.

- **Consistent with the changes in work, skills, and capabilities, organizational structures changed.** The number of people working at any given production location has been falling for seventy-odd years. Moreover, work is moving from line functions to staff; the proportion of people in staff positions has been rising for more than two hundred years. Finally, in the first three epochs, people typically worked as individuals, while during the two epochs before this one, they increasingly worked in ever more diverse teams. Today, the teams include people outside traditional manufacturing and engineering functions, such as sales and finance.

The critical organizational questions that we still must consider are: How will the diverse workgroups and people work together? What will the proportionately higher numbers of staff actually do? My overarching view is simple: *The staff will enable companies to build their businesses by linking the diverse workgroups.*

The Unfilled Role of Staff in an Adaptive Business

In prior epochs, people in staff positions served as the human drivers and coordinators of the work that arose from the technologies that powered the epochs. For example, during the Dynamic Control epoch, they anchored the focus on quality; they managed product testing, maintained the tools used to evaluate quality, and externally acquired raw materials and semifinished goods. During the Numeric Control epoch, the scope of staff work expanded even further. They became responsible for systems engineering, which included not only the traditional quality management of the prior epoch, but also the very design of the computer-driven production processes that were deployed.

It stands to reason, then, that in a world in which work is being performed by networks of workgroups within and outside individual companies, *the staff must ensure that the network of workgroups thrives*. I argued earlier that they will thrive only if the workgroups individually, and the network as a whole, develop and use three new capabilities—the ability to sense; the ability to respond; and the ability to learn, generalize, and share. This suggests that the staff must focus on creating, cultivating, and ultimately institutionalizing these new capabilities.

Yet *in virtually all companies today, no one is responsible for managing, nurturing, or leading these networks*. We have people assigned to every function from finance to human resources and top executives to lead them. We have become convinced that we need to manage processes, and we have assigned this task to yet more executives. For each of them, we have created entire departments and populated them with cadres of specialists. *But for the defining organizational characteristic of this epoch, we have nothing. Niemand. Personne. Nadie. Koi bhi nehi. May yo ren. Dare-mo-shitenai. No one is minding the store*.

The Chief Network Officer

Shouldn't someone? If networks are as important for corporate well-being as Nokia's experiences—and the other discussions in this book—indicate, it stands to reason that *someone* senior should actively manage them! This someone should be able to go toe-to-toe with other senior executives (in a win-win fashion, of course!) to ensure that the company adequately provides for the needs of its networks *and* the networks reciprocate by providing the value they should. Surely this would have happened as a matter of course if a more tangible, traditional resource had been involved?

The title I have assigned this senior executive is the *Chief Network Officer*. I know of no company, including Nokia, HP, and Toyota, that actually uses this title today. However, in a very few leading-edge companies, executives who have other formal titles and roles shoulder the CNO's responsibilities. At Nokia, Pertti Korhonen created the role, and Jean-Francois Baril stepped into his shoes.

The overarching responsibility of the CNO is to provide top management with the leadership to make his or her company adaptive. When I asked him for his opinion, Mr. Korhonen had no doubt that senior management had a critical role to play:

> It has to be a combination of top-down and bottom-up. If it is only bottom-up, there can be chaos or hundreds of initiatives that don't necessarily work together. There has to be a top-down message that this change is important, so that you can align the needles of the individual compasses, so that they all point to the North Pole.

The CNO must "align the needles of the individual compasses" by leading a company's efforts in five key areas:

- **Prospecting:** *Good* networks don't form by themselves; they have to be actively developed. A company may sense major changes in its market, technology, complementary resource, or supply environment and decide to modify its networks accordingly. As the global economy grows more complex, individual businesses may face such decisions regularly. Not every resource supplier needs to evolve beyond an arms-length transactional relationship, but anyone who provides a game-changing capability surely must. This cannot happen unless both sides are willing to invest time and effort in building a mutually productive relationship.

  These ideas collectively suggest that companies should constantly forage for potential partners who can not only provide key capabilities, but also can work effectively as partners. Mr. Baril considered this one of his primary responsibilities:

  > ...I have to understand who on the outside of Nokia is going to be key for us. Which people, which companies will support our business in the future? Which people and companies should clearly be in our network...so that we are able to get to 1 + 1 = 3?

- **Evangelizing:** In his book *The World Is Flat*, Thomas Friedman argues that in a world in which talented people can use computers to plug into the global economy, where they live no longer determines their fate.[1] Indeed, the unprecedented numbers of job options available globally is making talent retention a very difficult challenge for many companies. I know of two respected Fortune 100 companies that are facing double-digit annual turnover among professional staff and managers in China.

  What is true for talented people is also true of companies: where they are located no longer limits their prospects. How many people—even business executives—knew of Leveno before it bought IBM's personal computer business? How many had heard of Haier before it became a serious bidder for Maytag? How many had heard of Tata Steel till it took over Corus? How many had heard of Ranbaxy Laboratories or FoxConn? These names are simply the most recent, high-profile examples of an accelerating trend.

  The executives of these companies may not wear Oxford's or Cambridge's or Sandhurst's "old-school ties" or belong to Yale's Skull and Bones Society or have been Baker Scholars at Harvard Business School or have graduated from one of France's *Haute Ecoles*. But these companies are serious contenders for partnership roles, *and their executives know this well.* They can neutrally work for the highest bidder or monogamously contribute competitive edge to a network.

  The best CNOs must regularly evangelize their companies to not only choose the latter option, but to choose their own network and not another.[2] At Nokia, Mr. Baril's procurement and sourcing staff have prime responsibility for this task:

  > We were among the few people at Nokia who are in regular contact with the top executives of the high-tech industry.... We need to integrate them and their ideas into Nokia to contribute to transform Nokia. *Our fundamental role is to integrate the inside of Nokia to the outside. This may well define the basis of our mission for the next decade.*

  To this end, the CNO must work hard to develop *personal* relationships with top executives of potential and actual partners.

Mr. Baril often tells people that in his opinion, successful businesspeople must use their brains, heart, hands, and guts. In recent times, his current work has led him to add "a fifth element" for success: "...the mouth; you have to be able to communicate with people inside and outside."

- **Network building:** The CNO's third key task is actually building the network. *This is where all four of the Design Principles*—embedded sense and respond, win-win orientation, a bias for organizational learning, and use of appropriate technology—*interconnect*.

The CNO must answer two key questions. First, how will the outside and inside be interconnected so that the network works like a *virtual* company? You must consider how different workgroups inside and outside the company will work together. You also must consider what information needs to flow from whom to whom, when, how, and why. Mr. Baril suggested that "...the strength of the integration, with the best, highest levels of efficiency..." will be a key source of competitive advantage. Second, once the network is in place, how will it function in the face of unpredictable problems and challenges that will inevitably arise, such as a crippling fire at a key partner? Anticipating such issues and defining policies and processes to address them can provide the margin between success and failure.

- **Mediation:** Was I overreacting earlier when I wrote that "No one is minding the store?" One could argue that, to the contrary, marketing and sales take care of the market partners, R&D and legal take care of the technology partners, and supply chain and procurement take care of the supply partners. My response is that *even if these relationships are collaborative* (and most are not), *such an approach leaves unaddressed the fact that network partners often play multiple cross-functional roles*. As such, even if each function takes care of issues that it deems critical, *no one is responsible for the health of the overall relationship.*

As the four types of networks begin to overlap—this is itself a consequence of the blurring of industry boundaries—increasingly, *it will not make sense to artificially split them into neat, functionally focused bundles that assume that there are no impacts beyond intended boundaries ("externalities").* Externalities exist and have to be managed. For AutoCo, a good relationship with one buyer at a customer could not make up for the abusive behavior of the other buyers. At HP, concern about externalities led to the consolidation of relationship management first by the Buy-Sell program and then separately by the PRM program.

The person best suited to assuring the network's overall health is the CNO. He or she need not (and probably should not) manage all interactions a company has with all its partners on a day-to-day basis. He or she should represent the overall corporate interests, particularly when conflicts, *including those between partners, both internal and external*, arise.

* **Knowledge transfer:** All members of an adaptive organization must learn. The final role that the CNO must play is to ensure that good adaptive practices developed in one part of the organization are transferred to not just other parts, but, whenever appropriate, also across partner organizations. I will describe concrete elements of this role in the next chapter, while describing how a complex company can go about becoming an Adaptive Business. What is key is the fact that this task must continue long after the company has become comfortable with its adaptive capabilities.

Staffing the CNO's Office

Not long ago, I was describing the Chief Network Officer's role to a senior corporate lawyer. My friend observed, "Sounds to me like you are describing a Chief Operating Officer for *outside* the company." If one does not take this literally (the CNO in many situations will report to the COO), my friend's observation might not be a bad starting point for thinking about the role. Also implicit in my lawyer friend's observation is the idea that the CNO cannot do all the work I described himself or herself.

Indeed, when I asked Mr. Baril about his role, he immediately spoke of the need for a team. What is the appropriate structure of this team? I believe that there are two perfectly viable options:

- **Corporate:**   In relatively focused and/or centralized companies, a corporate team makes perfect sense. As long as its own application of the third Design Principle keeps it from becoming inward-focused, such an organization can drive adaptive principles quickly through the company.

- **Matrixed:**   In more complex environments, a strong matrix organization may be the best. This will probably be the preferred solution in most companies. A strong, core organization should define policy and coordinate action (particularly the transfer of learning) from the corporate level. Business unit level teams should be responsible for building the best Adaptive Business they can locally; they should report to both the business unit head and the corporate office. I have assumed this structure in Chapter 9, "Introduce Change Holographically," where I discuss implementation.

Finally, one may ask where the staff to support the CNO will come from. Ideally, the staff will be cross-functional. However, in all likelihood, many will have extensive experience in one of three functions that most have to deal with networks today: sales, R&D, and procurement. Which background will be more important will depend on the specific corporate situation. In companies where products are complex, procurement experience will be important. In companies where technology change is a key driver, R&D experience will be important. In companies where channels of distribution are complex or market conditions are highly competitive, sales experience will be critical.

Characteristics of a Strong Chief Network Officer

Whom should a company choose for this new role? Top executives should look among their senior staff for people who have three characteristics:

- **Business savvy:**   The CNO, first and foremost, needs to be a *business executive*, not a functional specialist. This person must understand the company's products, markets, competitors, technology, processes, and regulatory and socioeconomic environment. His or her mastery of these issues needs to be substantive; if it isn't, the CNO will not be able to find appropriate partners or improve processes. However, such mastery *alone* is not enough.

  While studying the world auto industry, Kim Clark and Takahiro Fujimoto noted that the senior executives who led major projects in the most effective R&D organizations were "multilingual translators."[3] They could *competently* talk to (for example) sales and marketing professionals in their own jargon and then explain their points *competently* to (for example) the R&D staff in the latter's own jargon. Each side felt that it had been understood, and better decisions came out of the process. The CNO must also have this capability; Mr. Baril described it as the ability "...to understand the business in a way that you will be respected by all functions..."

- **Collaborative nature:**   Leading a transformation requires dealing with a greater degree of complexity than simply overseeing "business as usual." In part this is because the CNO must turn the Design Principles into discrete, manageable actions that can be sustained over time, without interfering with the company's ability to function in the interim on the basis of traditional policies. In part, it is also because complexity is inherent in large, growing networks in which adding a single new participant adds many more links and flows (see Chapter 3, "Visions from the Present"). The default tendency will be to fall back into a plan-and-execute mode with its *illusion* of control, just when the right action might be to let decisions be made locally on a sense-and-respond basis.

  To deal with such complexity effectively, a CNO must have collaboration and consensus-building skills. When I was interviewing Mr. Korhonen, I had not yet formulated the role of the CNO, and I focused on the CEO as the transformative leader. I told Mr. Korhonen about some of the CEO transitions I documented in Chapter 5, "Succeed in a Dog-Eat-Dog World," and I asked his opinion about the early trends toward appointing collaborative individuals as CEOs. Mr. Korhonen replied that "...the CEO *must* be a consensus builder" or "the company gets left behind." However, the consensus could not be "false"; executives had to be free to disagree. He then added, *"The key thing is that it is done with respect, because then the arguing will lead to synthesis.* And the end result will develop into something much better." Mr. Korhonen's words are just as applicable to CNO candidates.

- **Imagination and a willingness to learn:**   The CNO must also be imaginative. He or she must be willing and able to visualize external and internal environments that are vastly different from the norm and, indeed, *seemingly* unreasonable. Without imagination, Mr. Korhonen said, "One's ability to see is limited by the horizon..." and solutions developed are not as far-reaching as they might otherwise have been.

  The CNO must also be willing to learn. At the beginning of an epoch, no one has a monopoly on knowledge. If the CNO does not have the humility to admit he or she does not have all the answers, the CNO will also find it hard to fashion innovative solutions. Indeed, I believe that a key reason why Mr. Korhonen succeeded as the point person for Nokia's transition was his willingness to admit he knew nothing about procurement or manufacturing or supply chains. "When you don't know something that you are responsible for," he told me, "it makes you humble, and you are forced into a learning mode."

  But *personally* having a bold imagination and being willing to learn is not enough. Mr. Baril described the difference between a great CNO and a good one:

  > The value of [Mr. Korhonen] was that if you talk to [Mr. Korhonen], everything becomes simple, and you look intelligent. *He creates the space for creativity.*

Final Thoughts on the Chief Network Officer

Taken together, the five facets of the CNO role and the three characteristics of good CNOs provide a simple test of whether a person is qualified to be a CNO: Is he or she on the short list of executives who have a realistic chance of reaching the top jobs in the company in the foreseeable future? If the answer is yes, he or she is qualified; if it is no, that person does not have the political and management skills needed for this challenging position. This criterion, however, *does not imply that the CNO position is a stepping-stone to the top.* Not every executive who dragged a major company kicking and screaming into the modern quality era became a CEO, and neither will every CNO.

So, You Are Not the CEO...

I often tell mid-career executives that they are at the cusp of their career. The focus of their job is changing from doing work—or managing work being done—to creating the conditions within which work is done. As such, unless you work for an autocratic company (which would probably never adopt the Adaptive Business model), you are empowered to heed Mr. Rosenberg's wisdom and build the organization that will build the (adaptive) business.

To do so, you must do the following:

1. Work to become "multilingual" yourself. This will require extensive interaction with other functions and disciplines and therefore will take time. To accelerate the process, join multi-functional project teams like the ones I discussed in Chapter 7, "Make Technology Matter." (Caveat: A team that operates as a collection of experts who push their own [function's] views instead of engaging in joint problem solving may not teach you much.)

2. Emulate Hewlett-Packard's mid-level managers. No CNO led them, but they still achieved much. In particular, the decision of the PRM group to behave like a start-up company that had to constantly sell itself was brilliant. Though the group focused on only the second Design Principle, it executed all five CNO tasks—prospect, evangelize, build networks, mediate, and transfer knowledge.

3. Analyze and change "decision rights." These define who has the authority to make (or not make) what decision under what circumstances. Doing so can often affect how work is done

(consider, for example, giving or taking away the power to approve overtime). Most mid-career executives have the authority to make such decisions, but few use it to drive organizational change. You should exercise this power; it may be as simple as changing a few words in a job posting. By doing so, *without senior management direction*, you can give your people some—or a lot of—authority to prospect, evangelize, build networks, mediate, and transfer knowledge. If you and a few of your peers jointly exercise this power to tackle the issues discussed in the "So You Are Not the CEO..." sidebars, you may be able to take your company a long way down the path of adaptive capabilities without top-management guidance.

Endnotes

[1]*The World Is Flat*, by Thomas Friedman, New York: Farrar Straus & Giroux, 2005.

[2]Incidentally, evangelizing is not a new idea; it has been practiced in the computer industry for at least twenty years. Guy Kawasaki, for example, wrote about his experiences as the "Chief Evangelist" for Apple's original Macintosh (*Rules for Revolutionaries*, Harper Collins, 1999). His job was to convince the vast numbers of independent companies that wrote software to write for the Macintosh operating system and not just for MS-DOS.

[3]*Product Development Performance*, by Kim Clark and Takahiro Fujimoto, Boston: Harvard Business School Press, 1991.

9

Introduce Change Holographically

For several years, I wrestled with the following question: Is adaptiveness a state or the journey? I have characterized Nokia and Toyota as adaptive companies and have left no doubt that EuroCo and the American auto companies are not. This dichotomous classification implicitly makes the case that adaptiveness is a state: either a business is adaptive, or it is not. But what of the sprawling empire that is HP, where some parts are clearly, well, and truly adaptive, and other parts—as quotes from HP executives indicate—are not there yet? What about Wal-Mart, which clearly does not have a win-win bone in its (metaphorical) body, but which, equally clearly, has used technologies to sense, respond, and learn more effectively than almost all other large companies? These two implicitly make the case for adaptiveness as a journey and allow us to consider one company more or less adaptive than another.

While the adaptiveness-as-a-state perspective is less realistic than adaptiveness as a journey, I have consciously adopted the former so far. The reason is simple: It can be tempting for an executive to point to isolated instances of the application of one or more of the Design Principles in his or her company and suggest that it is adaptive or is on the verge of becoming so. *Every* company can cite such examples; I would be surprised if even EuroCo executives couldn't.

Citing such examples is tantamount to believing that the path to adaptiveness resembles a hockey stick: A short period of hard, slow progress is followed by effortless, explosive growth. In reality, the path resembles a traditional "S curve," with a gently sloped middle section and an extended, relatively flat top. Initial growth will be slow and, yes, faster change will follow. But the critical step, beyond which adaptive capabilities will be "in the company's genes," is not the curve at the bottom but the *second* curve at the top. It takes time and sustained effort to implement all four Design Principles. A simple example from Nokia in 2000 supports this assertion. Recall Tapio Markki's statement that although he had to stop his meeting when he heard about the fire, he would not even pause a meeting today.

Creating an Adaptive Business

Assuming that we can switch perspectives from state to journey, how should a company embark on the task? Aside from the issue of time, I am certain about only one fact: There is no one right answer. Steps that may be perfect for one company may be disastrous for another. For example, building a technology-based sense-and-respond capability or a technology-based learning capability may be a lot easier than building collaborative relationships with network partners. Yet, I doubt that the U.S. auto companies would really benefit from these technologies if they did not work first on rebuilding relationships with their potential partners. With this important caveat, I have eight key recommendations for executives to consider.

Introduce Adaptive Transformation Holographically

In laypeople's terms, a hologram is a photograph that seems to give a three-dimensional representation of its subject. As an observer of the photo moves his or her position, the image in the photo seems to move in concert, as if the observer is in the presence of the photo's subject.

Decades after its invention, a hologram still dazzles us so much that few of us would consider cutting out a small piece of the image.

But if we did, we would find that in contrast to what would happen with a normal photograph, much of the entire original image would still be viewable, albeit from the perspective of the position occupied by the piece in the original photo.

The hologram is a marvelous metaphor for planning the adaptive transformation of a large, complex company. Imagine that a company is akin to the entire hologram and that each of its business units is one of the small pieces cut from it. We can then draw the following parallels:

- **Hologram:**   The complete image is a composite of each of the pieces; everything that is in each piece is in the complete image. **Companies:** The entire company is a sum of all its business units. Everything that exists in any business unit—policies, processes and culture, and environment—is a part of the overall company. However, all the rich detail that may be visible if we focus on any one part may be imperceptible in the whole.

- **Hologram pieces:**   Each piece has in it all the facets of the complete image. However, these facets are encoded within each piece from *the perspective of the piece*. **Business units:** Every business unit is affected by the policies, processes and culture, and environment of the overall company but has its own take on these, defined by its local needs and interpreted by local leaders and people. No business unit is identical to another; each is a good, but not faithful, representation of the overall company.

More large companies resemble the decentralized HP and not the cohesive, focused Nokia. As such, they should approach adaptive transformation *holographically*.[1] An adaptive implementation is holographic if it satisfies three conditions. First, policies adopted at the corporate level influence the transformation undertaken in any given business unit, even if they are not duplicated perfectly in any one. Second (and conversely), practices developed in each business unit have a core that is common across business units, but they also have a lot of local texture and color that is not relevant for any other and, indeed, may be detrimental to their health. Third, no individual business unit can put its faith in the hockey-stick model and declare victory early.

To approach their adaptive transformation holographically, companies must take three critically important steps:

- **Define the core policies at the corporate level.** This should be done even when a companywide transformation effort is not being—or cannot be—pursued all at once. The Chief Network Officer should be the custodian of this core—policies that should generally be treated as inviolable without the CNO's approval. Core policies, for example, might address screens for *consumer*-facing sense-and-respond capabilities, external sharing by one business unit of information that affects several, and incentive systems that affect corporate compensation. The CNO should also help the business units apply the core policies.

- **Introduce capabilities business unit by business unit, not Principle by Principle.** Studies in innovation and change management show that to overcome skepticism and gain broad acceptance, dramatically new ideas need to deliver discernable value. Since the four Design Principles reinforce each other, this suggests that companies that implement all the Design Principles methodically, business unit by business unit, are more likely to succeed than companies that try to introduce each Principle simultaneously across all business units. A business-unit-focused implementation would allow the reinforcing action to kick in far earlier than would be the case with a Design-Principle-focused implementation. The reinforcing action will help build momentum. Besides, the impact of problems that arise will be limited to a business unit, while the lessons learned in each unit can be applied across the company.

  The original application of adaptive principles at Nokia followed this model. Although CEO Jorma Ollila's goal was to transform all of Nokia, Pertti Korhonen started with the mobile phone unit. At HP, Venu Nagali's team learned one version of this lesson the hard way, while implementing the second Design Principle (PRM). Since their initial successes had been with memory chips, the team first tried to spread PRM across all of HP's chip purchases. Mr. Nagali said that although each such effort succeeded, they could not attract the senior management attention they needed to establish PRM as a valued corporate capability because "At the GM level, executives don't care about components." Three years ago, a switch to a business-unit-by-business-unit approach proved very valuable because:

> Doing deep dives lets you make trade-offs better.... when supply chain says, "We've never paid that much," Finance can say, "If you don't, you'll miss your targets." So we are able to optimize the business unit profitability.... You are helping the business unit make decisions that affect, say, $300 or $400 million.

- **Actively transfer lessons learned across business units.** The CNO must be responsible for transferring lessons learned at one business unit to other parts of the company and to external partners who might benefit. Some lessons may become a part of the corporate core; one cannot claim to believe in sense, respond, and learn if one refuses to leave the world of plan and execute! Other lessons will affect individual business units and speed up transformation for the entire network.

Pick a Business Unit That Wants to Change

In the 1990s, when I worked at the consulting company Arthur D. Little, I often had to convince businesses to take on transformational projects that defied traditional wisdom. I learned that it was easier to make the case to executives whose businesses were in the third to the fifth places in a competitive pecking order than to those who managed the leaders or the laggards. Executives at the leaders never thought they needed help, and those at the bottom often lacked the perspicacity or resources to engage in such projects.

This lesson—which I call the "B" player rule—is my primary criterion for selecting pilot sites for building adaptive capabilities. Even if the transformation is CEO-mandated and an effective CNO is in charge, efforts should begin in business units where support for change is high, not necessarily in those where the need is greatest or where business is doing well. These may often be business units that have had difficulty achieving their goals despite making concerted efforts or that recently have suffered serious, but not life-threatening, setbacks. They are more likely to try new ideas than those in turn-around situations or laggards, and they are also more likely to have the resources and the *human spirit* to make another run at winning.

When, then, is the best time to focus on a highflyer? Here it is important to differentiate between highflyers that are willing to rebuild their businesses regularly (like Nokia) and those that are on autopilot, loathe to experiment with anything that could potentially adversely affect their *perceived* sources of success. The former should be encouraged to jump in whenever they want. The latter are best approached when they feel threatened by the progress made by units that traditionally lagged them on some important performance metric. Finally, the real laggards should be approached last; if they go early and fail, they can scare off others.

Start at or Near the Top of the Organizational Hierarchy

Transforming an organization—as opposed to changing a few areas, even if critical—introduces many difficult challenges. Some are rational ("How should we improve interactions with customers?"), others are organizational ("We really need sales and logistics to jointly set policies for how to interact."), and yet others are political ("There must be a way of getting around those fellows in logistics. Give them a role now, and they will want one all the time."). The unfortunate fact of life is that more challenges fall into the second and third areas than the first.

Resolving such challenges often requires leadership by someone who has political clout; typically, this is someone senior. Indeed, without such backing, it may be hard to initiate and sustain a transformation in many companies (consider, for example, EuroCo). At a corporate level, the ideal sponsor is a CEO. (Particularly in America, Jean-Francois Baril opined, "...if you can get to the CEO, then you'll be able to touch everyone.") In any business unit, the top executive, or someone on his or her council, is essential. In the Nokia of 1995, both sorts of support were visible for Mr. Korhonen, who *de facto* played the role of the CNO. CEO Mr. Ollila provided visible, public corporate-level backing, while Matti Alahuhta, president of the Mobile Phone Division, provided support for the initial reform efforts that began there.

All is not lost in environments where such high-level support is unavailable, though undoubtedly the transformational effort becomes more difficult. Here, the efforts must be championed by impassioned, resolute managers who are true believers in adaptive principles. These managers need to dig in for the long haul *and think outside the box about how to gain broader acceptance of their effort*. For example, the awards that the PRM program won from unbiased external organizations helped raise its profile and credibility outside HP. In fact, years of such effort may also have helped within HP. For a while, at least one executive vice president held monthly one-on-one briefing sessions with Mr. Nagali; another interviewee said that although CEO Mark Hurd might not be involved, his direct reports discussed PRM regularly.

Build a Master Plan, Even One on a Small Scale

Ramchandran Jaikumar's epochal analysis is particularly compelling because it actually gives estimates of change that each epoch produced. Up to the fifth epoch, productivity (output per person-hour) rose by between 150% and 400% (typically, 300%), and quality improved between 20% and 75% (with greater improvement in more recent epochs). Since the second epoch, the number of products made in each facility rose substantially each time. With every epoch, the proportion of people in staff positions rose and reached 50%, while each of the last two epochs reduced staffing levels by about two-thirds. These improvements represent the cumulative actions of many tiny and big steps taken over years, perhaps as many as ten in the best-managed companies. Given the length of these trends, there is no reason not to expect them to continue for the foreseeable future.

Thus, these numbers provide guidelines for the overall extent of change that an adaptive transformation should produce. They in turn suggest *rough* targets for annual improvements at the corporate and/or business unit levels. For example, if we assume—based on prior experience—that the best-managed companies complete the transformation in a decade, each year productivity should rise about 12%, and quality should improve about 6%. These improvements may not be achievable in a given year, but appropriately compounded, they should be worthwhile targets over two- to three-year increments.

These will seem to be extraordinarily tough targets for most companies; without question, industry and economic conditions may require the adoption of gentler goals. The key point is this: the goals should not be overly gentle. Contrary to the suggestions of some, companies cannot transform by simply focusing their annual planning process on shorter-term objectives and developing a sharper focus on execution. Epochal changes produce step jumps in improvement; if the goals we set do not seem like step jumps, they probably do not reflect epochal change. If goals are not aligned with the magnitude of change that should be possible, the actual performance improvement that will be achieved will be disappointingly low.

Companies should augment this "Think big!" approach by taking a page from Toyota's playbook. They should approach the implementation of each element of the plan as an *experiment* in creating a new capability or changing a process or rethinking how to execute work. The company probably won't get everything right the first time. But if it truly decides to focus on learning, it will probably get it right the second or third time. Toyota's results—and Nokia's *largely organic* revenue growth of 550% over ten years—provide strong evidence that this approach can work.

Companies that do not pursue this approach will probably fall short of their capabilities. And the financial markets and analysts will bring out their grab bag of weapons and take aim at the CEO and other top executives. Some will then, in self-satisfied voices, proclaim victory for "aggressive shareholder capitalism," and others will shrug, say "Next!" in bored voices, and move on to making another financial killing by bringing down yet another group of executives.

Introduce the Design Principles in Waves

Adaptive capabilities should be built in three "waves," separated by periods of consolidation, as shown in Figure 9-1. Each wave should be invested with more intense effort than the prior one; the intervening periods of lowered intensity will enable the business to consolidate its gains. In each wave, a different Design Principle should be given prominence, while "appropriate chunks" of the others should provide support.

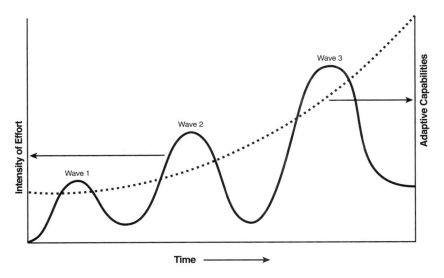

Figure 9-1   Introducing change in waves

Nothing in life is free. The wave-based approach will probably require more time than an all-out assault. Undoubtedly, the greatest benefits will be achieved only after the third wave is under way. However, this approach reduces the complexity that the business must manage. Indeed, the initial efforts during each wave should also be limited to one or two challenges (see the next section) and should be broadened only as success and experience accrue.

The first wave should focus on sense-and-respond capabilities, as shown in Table 9-1. Both Nokia and HP went down this path in the early years of their transformational efforts. This will require the organization to divide its attention between its external and internal environments. To make sense-and-respond work, businesses should inject just as much of a win-win orientation and technology as are necessary. Analytical skills are good to have, but not critical at this stage; indeed, excessive efforts directed at these will draw attention away from the company's external world. Nokia took these steps too, relying on its culture of learning to see it through this wave.

TABLE 9-1   Composition of the Waves

	Wave 1	**Wave 2**	**Wave 3**
Focus	Mixed: external and internal	Internal	External
Primary Goal	Sense and respond	Organizational learning	Win-win
Secondary Goal	Win-win, technology for sense and respond	Sense and respond, technologies for organizational learning, and sense and respond	Organizational learning, sense and respond, and technologies for all
Tertiary Goal	Organizational learning	Win-win	

In Wave 2, the focus should shift *internally* to creating organizational learning capabilities. This perspective may seem to contradict the arguments about a networked world, but it simply recognizes that a business cannot do well externally without preparing itself internally. Wave 2 is critical since—as I argued in Chapter 6, "Ensure That Work Teaches"—the capabilities it brings to the business are necessary for evaluating what is being sensed and also for determining when the sense-and-respond system as a whole must change. One is essential in the short run, and the other in the medium term. *Really* good analysis also helps a business determine the partners with which it *must* build win-win relationships.

During Wave 3, a business should develop *enduring* win-win relationships with its major partners. Doing so gets it past the top of the "S curve" that I discussed at the beginning of this chapter. That is why Table 9-1 lists no tertiary goal for Wave 3: At the top, everything is important.

Throughout this book, I have implied that HP, a company for which I have great respect, is, as of this writing, still in the process of institutionalizing the adaptive approach to business. At this point, I can actually explain why. Whereas Nokia has integrated all the Design Principles as presented in Wave 3, HP has developed each of these Design Principles but has not yet integrated them into a system. To achieve the next level of excellence, HP will have to move the application of the Design Principles from thoughtful action to unconscious routines and embed them in its culture.

Start with the Non-Customer-Facing Ends

Wherever possible, companies should start the transformation with initiatives in areas that do not immediately touch customers— particularly consumers. Dealing with consumers can be complex, and the temptation to use the power of technology to sense and respond is seductive (see Chapters 4 and 7). This can be a volatile mixture for a company that is dipping its metaphorical toe into the adaptive lake. Adaptive capabilities can be far more easily developed and deployed with technology-creating, supply-assuring, and complementary-resource-developing partners. Working on these first will teach the company a lot about the nuts and bolts of how it can best deploy sense and respond for customers.

The only exception to this recommendation is when a customer initiates an adaptive effort. In such cases, businesses should respond positively with a senior executive-led cross-functional team focused on the customer. This team *must not* simply focus on sense-and-respond capabilities or technologies that enable these, as could be the case if the customer were Wal-Mart or Germany's Metro AG or the U.S. government. Instead, this team should design a "mini adaptive business" focused solely on the customer. Moreover, this team must seriously document the lessons it learned for wider application in the business.

Remember That Incentives Can Be an Executive's Best Friend

Executives, particularly the Chief Network Officer, need to ensure that incentive systems that are in place do not cause people to act against the Design Principles. This is particularly true at the business unit level. Nokia had, as I mentioned earlier, changed incentives to ensure that its staff were forced to think cross-functionally, while HP acknowledged that its effort to implement PRM broadly had been slowed by the absence of a performance measurement system that took into account *all* product costs.

For the Foreseeable Future, Let the Results Speak for Themselves

In the late 1990s, a major American manufacturer decided to adopt Lean Sigma. The company's plants were decades behind the state of the art; some did not even have simple assembly lines, let alone sophisticated management systems. Anyone with any knowledge of Lean Sigma would have known that it would be many years before the company saw benefits. The discounted cash flow values of these benefits probably would have had a negligible impact on the company's EPS. But this did not matter. The company's CEO, a superb marketer, invited a group of financial analysts and reporters to visit one of the company's factories and personally announced the Lean Sigma program to them. His marketing smarts paid off; the analysts and journalists wrote glowing articles about the initiative and, starting the day after the factory visit, the share price began rising.

Adaptive Business has the power to help companies thrive. However, it is still years away from having the power to influence financial markets, as did the adoption of Lean by the American manufacturer just mentioned. This is actually a good thing! By introducing change under the radar of the financial markets, companies may make it easier for change to take hold. As such, CEOs who decide to take their companies down this path should leave the flamboyance to those who will follow them.

Some Final Thoughts

I want to end this chapter where I began it: very few things in management have one right answer. My job has been to present a new approach to managing for the world of networked companies and to give examples of how leading companies are tackling the challenge. The job of every executive should be to determine how best to lead the transformation in his or her company. The choices a CEO makes must take into account more rational, organizational, and political issues than any book can cover. All I can add is, be prepared for a roller coaster ride. If you get on a roller coaster willingly, you know that sheer exhilaration trumps your fright and stomach-in-the-mouth feelings. Such is the case here. At the end, as after most roller coaster rides, you will have a broad smile on your face.

So, You Are Not the CEO...

Years ago, at the INSEAD business school, I used to quote Professor Andrew Van de Ven: "New ideas that are not considered useful are not called innovations. They are called mistakes." After my students' laughter died down, I would say, "This funny statement is actually profound. It says that a great idea may be ignored if it is deemed unusable. So, what conditions drive usability?"

Since those times, I have led teams that have modified technologies, created next-generation products, developed new standard operating processes, trained staff, managed product launches, led people, and done a host of things that most good, dependable, practicing managers do daily. So I understand that the demands of the real world can easily keep the most well-intentioned manager, professional, or executive from actually applying lessons learned. But the sad truth is, Professor Van de Ven was right. No implementation, no change, no superb performance, no currency, no glory. *So, if the ideas in this book make sense, find an opportunity, however small, to implement them to whatever extent you can.*

If you work in an operating unit and your corporate executives are oblivious to the need for change, implement the ideas in your unit alone. In this case, ignore my discussion of corporate policies and mandates. The B-player rule suggests that when you have changed your unit, others will notice. And if they do not, you will be positioned to take your experiences to another employer who will let you build a great adaptive business.

If you work at headquarters, you have two options. If your position allows you to play the *de facto* role of the Network Officer (I deliberately left out "Chief"), by all means, assume it and help your colleagues in the operating units move more quickly. If not, seek a transfer to a B-player unit where you can apply the ideas. Simply sitting in the rarified atmosphere of a corporate office thinking about adaptiveness will not help your company.

In the operating units:

- Fly under the radar as long as you can. Not getting a thousand attaboys may seem unfair, but deferred praise may be worth the wait (though I will not guarantee it).

- Think big when you build your master plan. Recently, a successful top executive told an executive education class I was teaching, "People often do not realize that it takes almost as much effort to achieve small goals as big ones. Go for the big ones!"

- Manage your risk by limiting the scope of your effort to (for example) one or two key products or customers rather than the entire portfolio of your operating unit.

- Adopt the three waves approach, unless unimpeachable factors oppose doing so. In a relatively controlled arena, you may capture tangible benefits with the first wave.

- Proactively address organizational and political challenges. Use incentives to drive behavior, and never forget: *Nothing of importance gets done solely through formal lines of authority*.

Good luck!

Endnote

[1]Only about a third of HP's total spending on components and products is centrally managed. This means that for any major change, many executives have to be individually convinced.

Epilogue: Two Views of a Company

I interviewed Pertti Korhonen on a beautiful spring day in 2006. The weather had just started turning warm—this is a relative term in Finland—and the afternoon was brilliantly sunlit. I was still thinking about the interview as I walked up to Nokia's front desk and asked for a taxi. A young woman who reached the desk right after I did overheard my request and introduced herself as a Nokia employee. She asked if I would consider sharing the taxi, and I agreed.

In the taxi, she promptly informed me that she had just completed her first month at Nokia after spending several years in another organization abroad. I did not tell her about my visit, and she did not ask. Instead, I asked her, "How do you like it?" A wondrous look came over her face. "I just don't understand it," she said. "People are so friendly and cooperative. It's like they want to work together. They share information and ideas with you. That was not like where I was." She paused before adding, "Of course, I've only been here a month. I could find out in time it is really not like that."

Another pause followed. Then she said, "The other thing is, people are so excited and interested in working on new projects, to try different things. I mean, we are all very busy. But still, if you propose anything new, they are totally willing to try it, take on another project. That's not what I am used to." She paused again before continuing. "Of course, I am new here, and that could change."

I asked, "Is it hierarchical?" She responded with some passion, "Not at all hierarchical!... Of course, that could just be the Finnish culture. I'm Finnish, but have not lived here for nine years. Finns are not hierarchical. Maybe that's what it is!"

Immediately after we parted at the airport, I pulled out my computer and documented her words as closely as I remembered them.

I'm sure many current and ex-employees will argue that my co-traveler painted a Pollyannaish picture of Nokia, and that I "fell for it." Maybe they are right, for we are human, after all, and no human organization is perfect. However, she put a smile on my face that lasted the rest of the day. Our meeting was coincidental, so it is hard to see how she could have had a vested agenda. In this era of extreme cynicism, it was refreshing to hear someone reflect the picture of Nokia that Mr. Korhonen had drawn for me.

❈ ❈ ❈

At the time I was having this serendipitous conversation, Nokia was undergoing a major transition. Several top executives, including CEO Jorma Ollila, Matti Alahuhta, and Mr. Korhonen, were stepping down in what seemed to be an orderly, planned changing of the guard. Could the Design Principles survive such a broad change in leadership?

Because of the words of Olli-Pekka Kallasvuo, Nokia's new president and CEO, I believe they have. For its January 2007 issue, the *Harvard Business Review* asked a diverse group of business leaders what they thought was *the most important* leadership quality.[1] Others wrote about issues that ranged from the mundane (keep bureaucracy at bay, have good judgment) to issues I have discussed here (be passionate). Mr. Kallasvuo wrote about the need for *humility*:

> Humility is a vital quality in a leader, just as it is for a company. Nokia, if it is to continue to prosper...has to be humble in the face of complexity.... [It] can't be so overconfident as to believe its predictions are the best. Instead, *we need to perceive changes as they occur and react the fastest.* In a management team, that responsiveness is a product of diversity—managers must humbly accept that their own perspectives need to be broadened by others'.
>
> ...you appreciate how much you depend on others—another humbling realization. When I was first put in charge of a team 19 years ago, I had to come to terms with the fact that I was

no longer a lone professional doing my own job. I had to manage in such a way that other people would be the ones making things happen, not me. With every year, the lesson has intensified...*there's very little I can do alone. But there is much I can do with the team* (italics added throughout the excerpt).

So, the baton has been passed successfully. Managing for the good of the network is well ingrained, not just as a matter of strategy, but as a bedrock principle of good management. Nokia continues to be an environment in which a top executive can say without any self-consciousness that Antoine de St. Exupery's *Le Petit Prince* can teach managers a lot. It is also an environment in which the CEO feels no qualms about publicly pronouncing humility as *the most important* leadership quality. Finally, Nokia still encourages, as I have documented, risk-taking to reshape the business completely. As I write this in mid-2007, Nokia is reentering the Internet gaming business after bombing in this market as recently as 2005. The interim financial results for 2007 continue to prove that this managerial approach is still benefiting customers, shareholders, and the communities in which Nokia is based.

I am sure that Nokia, like any other Adaptive Business, will face normal ups and downs in its business fortunes in the years ahead. I am equally sure that the Design Principles will help them rebound from the downs and re-create work environments that enthuse people like my co-passenger in the Helsinki taxi.

Endnote

[1]"Moments of Truth: Global Executives Talk About the Challenges That Shaped Them as Leaders," *Harvard Business Review*, January 2007, pp. 15–25.

INDEX